Backup and Restore Practices
for Sun Enterprise™ Servers

Stan Stringfellow
Miroslav Klivansky
with **Michael Barto**

Sun Microsystems Press
A Prentice Hall Title

The publisher offers discounts on this book when ordered in bulk quantities. For more information, contact: Corporate Sales Department, Phone: 800-382-3419; Fax: 201-236-7141; E-mail: corpsales@prenhall.com; or write: Prentice Hall PTR, Corp. Sales Dept., One Lake Street, Upp Saddle River, NJ 07458.

Editorial/Production Supervisor: *Nicholas Radhuber*
Cover Design Director: *Jerry Votta*
Cover Designer: *Kavish & Kavish Digital Publishing & Design*
Manufacturing Manager: *Alexis R. Heydt*
Marketing Manager: *Bryan Gambrel*
Acquisitions Editor: *Greg Doench*

Sun Microsystems Press:
Marketing Manager: *Michael Llwyd Alread*
Publisher: *Rachel Borden*

10 9 8 7 6 5 4 3 2 1

ISBN 0-13-089401-X

Sun Microsystems Press
A Prentice Hall Title

Acknowledgments

It is remarkable that so many talented and busy people were willing to take the time to contribute to the making of this book. I am very grateful to all of them.

Miroslav Klivansky, who manages the Storage Performance Engineering group at Sun Microsystems, contributed what is surely the intellectual core of this book, Chapter 4, "Methodology: Planning a Backup Architecture." He wrote other smaller sections as well. Coauthorship credit was well deserved.

Michael Barto, a technologist for Sun Microsystems Professional Services, contributed the content for Chapter 5, "NetBackup Runbook." Michael is known for his work in creating runbooks for Sun's professional services organization, and his contribution helped to round out this book.

Special thanks to Richard Elling, a senior engineer with the Sun Enterprise Engineering group, for developing and writing the "Simple Sizing Model" in Chapter 4.

In the Sun BluePrints program, we want to work with customers to cross-pollinate and disseminate best practices information. The folks at Qualcomm Incorporated were remarkably helpful on this front.

Brian Vogelsang, Senior Engineer and Manager of Enterprise Systems at Qualcomm, is very well versed in backup and restore issues and was willing to take the time to answer a whole lot of questions. His insights contributed mightily to the usefulness of this book.

Neal Sundberg, a staff DBA at Qualcomm, is another one of those guys who pretty much knows all there is to know. He was helpful and friendly and took the time to update and contribute the Oracle Parallel Export script, described in Chapter 6. This, despite the birth of twins during the process. Congratulations Neal! Also, thanks to Mike Ellison of Qualcomm who wrote the original version of the Oracle Parallel Export script.

Kevin Hagen, a staff DBA at Qualcomm, was also quite helpful and provided many useful insights.

Ravishankar (Ravi) Govendarajan, of the Production Service Center Tools Group at Sun Microsystems, was always enthusiastic. He provided guidance and useful information, despite a very busy schedule.

Chuck Hellier and Brian Cinque of Sun Microsystems also provided useful insights into several backup and restore issues, and I appreciate their time.

Credit belongs to Harris Kern, Randy Johnson, Michael W. Hawkins, and Andrew Law, whose book *Managing the New Enterprise* (Prentice Hall, 1996) was helpful in developing the "Backup Tool Selection Criteria" section in Chapter 1.

On the partnership front, special thanks to Ann Sheridan, Director of Marketing at VERITAS Software Corporation, and Dale Hanson, a marketing manager at VERITAS.

Thanks to everyone who reviewed the book, including Jack Bochsler, Ed Darrah, Don DeVitt, Mary Ferguson, Ed Gamble, Dennis Henderson, Sue Jackson, John Lazarus, Ranna Patel, and Anola Saycocie. I hope I haven't forgotten anyone.

And, finally, here at home... Thanks to the very talented folks in Sun's Enterprise Engineering group, including John Howard, Richard McDougall, Bill Sprouse, and Enrique Vargas who provided guidance and reviews. Thanks to technical writers Terry Williams and David Gee. Also, thanks to Barb Jugo, BluePrints Publications Manager, and Chuck Alexander, Manager of Enterprise Engineering, for letting me do such a fun job.

Stan Stringfellow, June 2000

Contents

Chapter 2 - Backup and Restore Basics

Chapter 3 - Case Studies

Chapter 4 - Methodology: Planning a Backup Architecture

Chapter 5 - NetBackup Runbook

Chapter 6 - Oracle Parallel Export Script

Preface

Backup and Restore Practices for Sun Enterprise Servers focuses on technologies available from Sun Microsystems, Inc., and includes detailed information on backup and restore practices using software products and Sun Enterprise™ servers running the Solaris™ operating environment.

This book takes a multifaceted approach to the topic and includes case studies developed from interviews with IT staff at companies who run their core operations on Sun Enterprise servers. It also contains a thorough and detailed methodology for planning and implementing a backup and restore architecture. To assist in the standardizing of daily backup and restore operations, appropriate sections of the book provide step-by-step procedures in runbook format.

Who Should Use This Book

This book is intended for IT managers, system administrators, and database administrators involved in planning and implementing a backup and restore architecture in a networked environment using Sun Microsystems™ technologies.

How This Book Is Organized

Chapter 1, "Managing a Backup and Restore Initiative,"provides a high-level overview of backup and restore issues from the managerial point of view. The chapter includes a detailed description of the issues to be considered when purchasing a backup and restore software tool.

Chapter 2, "Backup and Restore Basics," provides a technical overview of the backup and restore technologies used within modern networked environments.

Chapter 3, "Case Studies," presents case studies dealing with issues involved in planning and implementing a backup and restore architecture. These case studies can help broaden your understanding on a wide range of related topics.

Chapter 4, "Methodology: Planning a Backup Architecture," presents a thorough and detailed methodology to use when planning and implementing a backup and restore architecture. This information can be useful when formulating plans or proposals for submission to management and can serve as a reference guide during the implementation phase.

Chapter 5, "NetBackup Runbook," provides step-by-step procedures, in runbook format, that can be helpful in environments using Sun StorEdge Enterprise NetBackUp™ software. Runbooks can be useful for standardizing and simplifying the day-to-day operations throughout an IT organization.

Chapter 6, "Oracle Parallel Export Script," describes a script contributed by Qualcomm, Inc., that significantly speeds up Oracle database exports on symmetric multiprocessing (SMP) machines. This script can enhance your options when performing regularly scheduled parallel exports of large databases that must be continuously available. The approach can deliver important benefits, including faster and less intrusive restores, and is a valuable addition to the standard "best practices" associated with an Oracle backup.

Appendix A, "High-Speed Database Backups on Sun Systems," describes a benchmark study that demonstrated backup speed of more than a terabyte per hour with Sun technologies. The demonstration was performed jointly by Sun Microsystems, VERITAS Software Corp., Oracle Corp., and Storage Technology Corp. (STK).

Appendix B, "Business Continuity Planning and Sun Technologies," provides a brief overview of Sun technologies that are applicable to business continuity planning and disaster recovery. For additional information on these topics, see the Sun BluePrints™ book, *Business Continuity Planning with Sun Microsystems Technologies*.

Using UNIX Commands

This document does not contain information on basic UNIX® commands and procedures such as shutting down the system, booting the system, and configuring devices.

See one or more of the following for this information:

- *AnswerBook2™ online documentation for the Solaris operating environment.*
- Other software documentation that you received with your system.

Typographic Conventions

Typeface	Meaning	Examples
AaBbCc123	The names of commands, files, and directories; on-screen computer output	Edit your `.login` file. Use `ls -a` to list all files. `% You have mail.`
AaBbCc123	What you type, when contrasted with on-screen computer output	`% `**`su`**` Password:`
AaBbCc123	Book titles, new words or terms, words to be emphasized	Read Chapter 6 in the *User's Guide*. These are called *class* options. You *must* be superuser to do this.
	Command-line variable; replace with a real name or value	To delete a file, type `rm` *filename*.

Shell Prompts

Shell	Prompt
C shell	*machine_name*%
C shell superuser	*machine_name*#
Bourne shell and Korn shell	$
Bourne shell and Korn shell superuser	#

Accessing Sun Documentation Online

The `docs.sun.com` Web site provides access to Sun technical documentation online. You can browse the `docs.sun.com` archive or search for a specific book title or subject. The URL is

`http://docs.sun.com/`

Additional information related to backup and restore issues is available from the SunUP™ program at:

`http://www.sun.com/availability`

Ordering Sun Documentation

Fatbrain.com, an Internet professional bookstore, stocks select product documentation from Sun Microsystems, Inc.

For a list of documents and how to order them, visit the Sun Documentation Center on Fatbrain.com at:

`http://www1.fatbrain.com/documentation/sun`

Sun Welcomes Your Comments

Sun is interested in improving its documentation and welcomes your comments and suggestions. You can send email with your comments to Sun at:

`docfeedback@sun.com`

Please include the part number (806-2894-10) of this book in the subject line of your email.

## CHAPTER 1

Managing a Backup and Restore Initiative

Sun and the Evolving Datacenter Model

Organizations today are reaching beyond the traditional glass house boundaries to interact directly with customers, partners, suppliers, and employees. In this new extended enterprise model, organizations seek to provide universal access to information and services through business portals on the World Wide Web. This shift, born out of the pressure of global competition in a networked world, places new availability, manageability, and performance requirements on a datacenter. Today's IT priorities include improving business processes, improving customer data quality, developing better customer relationship management, implementing high availability networks, boosting networking bandwidth, and building e-commerce infrastructures.

In this evolving business paradigm, new data is generated at exponential rates and plays a more vital and publicly visible role than ever before. Consequently, organizations must place a high priority on safeguarding mission-critical data and ensure it remains continuously available. A reliable, flexible, and highly scalable network-based backup and restore solution is an essential part of this endeavor.

Sun Microsystems, Inc., supports the new business model with enterprise servers, storage products, networking hardware, and related software and services, including leading backup and restore solutions. For up-to-date information on Sun™ datacenter initiatives, see

    http://www.sun.com/datacenter.

For information on services available from Sun, including professional consulting services, see

    http://www.sun.com/service.

Sun offers a line of enterprise servers, from the Sun Enterprise Ultra™ 5S up to the mainframe-class Sun Enterprise™ 10000, also known as the Starfire™ server. At the time of this writing, Sun has shipped well over 1000 Starfire servers, which are now operating in 46 countries worldwide. Many datacenters are powered entirely by Sun Enterprise servers, similar to those shown in FIGURE 1-1.

FIGURE 1-1   Starfire Servers Deployed in a Datacenter

High availability is a major component of Sun datacenter initiatives. SunUP is a collaborative program between Sun, customers, and third parties to analyze, develop, implement and manage services, infrastructure, and products that improve availability. For additional information, see

http://www.sun.com/availability

Genesys is the Sun code name for the platform architecture of datacenter dot com, the new datacenter model. Genesys is also a program, consisting of products and services, aimed at helping IT organizations move their datacenters into the dot com era. For additional information about Genesys, see

http://www.sun.com/datacenter/genesys.html

Sun has received the attention and enthusiasm of today's software developers. Many of the new Internet-enabled applications are written for the Solaris Operating Environment and optimized for Sun systems. Sun is the platform of choice for enterprise resource planning (ERP), electronic commerce, and database/data warehousing applications, as well as server consolidation initiatives.

The Sun-Netscape Alliance, known as iPlanet (http://www.iplanet.com), also supports the portal computing model with software and services—as well as content and audience reach through the AOL/Netscape end of the alliance. The Sun-Netscape Alliance offers a full range of software products, including the NetDynamics™ application server, the highest-performance application server on the market.

To support the new datacenter model, large organizations must employ a backup and restore solution that can scale massively in a widely distributed environment. To help customers meet this demand, Sun offers OEM versions of the two most popular and powerful enterprise backup and restore tools on the market: VERITAS NetBackup as Sun StorEdge Enterprise NetBackUp™, and Legato Networker™ as Solstice Backup™.

There are many other backup and restore products on the market, but these two are among the most scalable and robust products available. Choosing a backup and restore tool is one of the most important decisions an IT manager must make. For guidance on this issue, see "Backup Tool Selection Criteria" on page 6.

Note – This book uses the name NetBackup when referring to the VERITAS NetBackup product.

Modern developments in backup technology require significant processing power and I/O bandwidth. Sun Enterprise servers provide scalable symmetric multi-processing, from 1 to 64 high-performance UltraSPARC™-II processors, with up to 64 Gbytes of memory and up to 20 Tbytes of disk storage. The advent of scalable I/O platforms such as these enables a database to be configured for the optimal balance of processing power and I/O bandwidth, so online backups can proceed with minimal impact on database performance.

Note – The Sun StorEdge™ Instant Image and Sun StorEdge Network Data Replicator products are not covered in this book. For information on these products, see the BluePrints book: *Business Continuity Planning for Sun Microsystems Technologies*.

The NetBackup GUI, shown in FIGURE 1-2, supports centralized administration of a backup and restore architecture that may include widely distributed nodes located throughout a global enterprise.

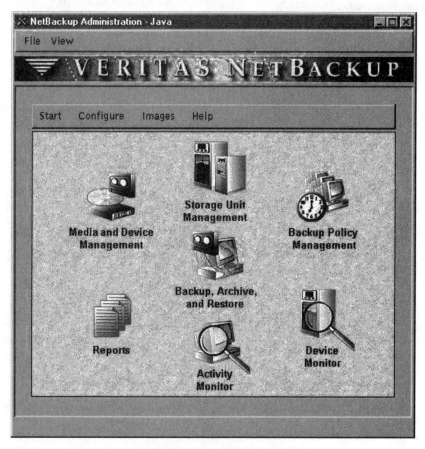

FIGURE 1-2   Java™ technology version of the NetBackup GUI

Managerial Issues

Implementing a backup and restore architecture scalable enough to meet current and future business needs requires broad support for the project. Depending on the organizational structure of the business, a diverse set of people and interests will need to be brought onboard. The cooperation and approval from different VPs, business units, and operational groups may be required.

Some of the following groups could be involved:

- Systems administrators—The persons responsible for planning and implementing backup and restore solutions.

- Database administrators—Including DBAs inside and outside the datacenter.

- Application development groups—Those responsible for developing internal applications and customizing purchased enterprise applications.

- Operations personnel—Those responsible for day-to-day operations of the backup and restore tools.

The system administrators and the database administrators must work together to define responsibilities. The DBAs will want to retain control over database backup and restore procedures. The system administrators will define the ways that file systems are backed up, including files that are created when databases are exported for backup purposes. These two groups should work together to define the backup and restore architecture, evaluate and test the backup and restore tool that will be used, customize the backup and restore tool, and define the operational lines of responsibility.

The mainframe and client/server system administrators need to work together. These two groups should be integrated as much as possible, rather than separated into distinct realms. Integration can increase trust and cooperation.

Negotiations can be carried out to determine service levels for each business unit. Address such issues as how long backed up data must be kept online, which data is critical and which is not, what the backup timeframe will be, and other details. (See "TechEvolve Corp. Case Study" on page 27, for more information on negotiations.) Set up service levels with the various business units and formalize into service-level agreements. The customers of the IT services need to pay for what they are receiving, since service levels imply human, software, and hardware resource costs.

In a rapidly growing enterprise, there may already be an established backup and restore infrastructure and set of procedures; however, the current architecture may no longer be suitable. Several different backup and restore tools may be in use, either purchased or developed in-house. Eventually these tools could reach their limitations in terms of scalability or may become too unwieldy to handle the growing needs of the enterprise.

The solution is to consolidate under a highly scalable toolset and architecture. All groups using the legacy tools will need to agree on their use to make this consolidation successful. This agreement could involve tradeoffs, so everyone involved should be informed of the overall goals. For example, a backup and restore tool developed in-house might serve some purposes well and might be easy to customize for certain groups. But the tool may need to be replaced with a standardized tool in the interest of overall efficiency. Everyone involved should understand the larger goals and be prepared to make some concessions if necessary.

To successfully implement a new backup and restore architecture, develop a plan based on the guidelines in Chapter 4, "Methodology: Planning a Backup Architecture" on page 61. All parties affected by the transition should be involved in developing, approving, and implementing the plan.

Backup Tool Selection Criteria

Choosing a backup and restore tool is one of the most important decisions to be made. The entire backup and restore architecture will be built around that tool. The features and development direction of the tool should be evaluated in light of your current and future business requirements. In your evaluation, consider the stability of tool vendors, quality of their service, and level of technical support.

The following section covers a wide range of selection criteria that you should consider when purchasing a backup tool.

Architectural Issues

The architecture of a backup tool is extremely important. The entire backup and restore infrastructure can be enhanced or limited by the architecture of the underlying tool.

Ask the following questions:

- *Does the architecture scale to support your current and future needs?*

  NetBackup and Solstice Backup use hierarchical architecture. Hierarchical architecture simplifies the addition of nodes to a network of backup servers and aids in structuring backup architecture appropriately for a particular organization. For example, a global enterprise may have several datacenters around the world in which master backup servers can be located. With hierarchical architecture, it is easy to add and delete slave backup servers beneath each master. This architecture can therefore be scaled to a global level, while still providing required flexibility.

- *Is SAN support provided?*

  A storage area network (SAN), is a high-speed, dedicated network that establishes a direct connection between storage devices and servers. This approach allows storage subsystems, including tape subsystems, to be connected remotely. Tape SANs enable the sharing of tape resources efficiently among many servers. Both the backup and restore tool and tape library must provide SAN support to make this sharing possible.

  With a SAN, information can be consolidated from increasingly remote departments and business units than was previously possible. This approach enables the creation of centrally managed pools of enterprise storage resources. Tape resources can be migrated from one system on a SAN to another, across different platforms.

  SANs also make it possible to increase the distance between the servers that host data and tape devices. In the legacy model, tape devices that are attached through a SCSI interface are limited to 25 meters. With fiber-channel technology, distances of up to 10 kilometers can be supported. This makes it possible to use storage subsystems, including tape devices, in local or remote locations to improve the storage management scheme and to offer increased security and disaster protection.

Note – At the time of this writing, tape SANs are not a viable solution for production environments. However, planning for a tape SAN will ensure your backup and restore architecture is well positioned to transition to this technology as it becomes production-ready.

- *Can backups to remote devices be made?*

  If a server hosts a small amount of data (less than 20 Gbytes), it can be more convenient to back up over the standard network. Traditional network backups can be chosen in some cases.

Remote and Global Administration

Any widely distributed organization needs to centrally manage and remotely administer the backup and restore architecture.

Ask the following questions:

- *Does the tool support centralized administration?*

  The VERITAS Global Data Manager (GDM) utility supports the concept of a global data master. This master-of-masters server enables central control of a set of master backup servers located anywhere in the world.

- *Does the tool support remote administration?*

  The tool should support all capabilities from any location, including dial-up or low bandwidth networks.

- *Is electronic client installation available?*

  The tool should support fast, easy software distribution of backup client agents.

- *Is backup progress status available?*

  The completion time of a backup should be available, and so should the amount of data backed up so far and the remaining data to be backed up.

- *Can historical reporting logs be browsed?*

  The tool should support an in-depth analysis of prior activity.

- *Does the tool provide disaster recovery support?*

  It should be possible to recover data remotely across the network.

- *Are unattended restore operations supported?*

  The tool should support unattended restore of individual files, complete file systems, or partitions.

- *Are unattended backups supported?*

  Can the tool schedule and run unattended backups? A backup tool generally has a built-in scheduler, or you can choose a third-party scheduler. Large organizations commonly use a third-party scheduler, since many jobs, not just backups, need to be scheduled. A greater level of control is offered by the script-based scheduling approach. If using a third-party tool, ensure the backup tool has a robust command-line interface and the vendor is committed to backward compatibility in future versions of the commands that control the execution of the backup tool.

Automation

Backup process automation is essential in any large organization since it is impractical to run backup jobs manually. The effectiveness of the entire backup and restore architecture depends on the automated support provided by the backup tool.

Ask the following questions:

- *Does the tool support automation of system administration?*

  The tool should provide a robust set of APIs that enable customizing and automation of system administration. The API should allow customization by using standard or commonly accepted scripting language such as Bourne shell, Perl, or Python.

■ *Is there a GUI-based scheduler?*

It should be easy to define schedules, set backup windows, and identify backups with meaningful names.

High Availability

If the data source must be highly available, then the backup and restore tool needs to support that requirement. This means both the tool and the data it manages must be highly available.

Ask the following questions:

■ *Is the backup tool itself highly available?*

This requirement involves not only the backup and restore tool, but also the servers on which the tool runs. In a master–slave architecture, the master and slave software and hardware servers may need to be designed with redundant systems with failover capabilities. Consider also the availability requirements of the desktop systems and backup clients.

■ *What are backup retention requirements?*

Determine how long tape backups need to be retained. If backing up to disk files, determine the length of time backup files need to be retained on disk. The media resources needed to satisfy these requirements depend on the retention times and the volume of data being generated by the business unit.

■ *Does the tool ensure media reliability?*

The backup and restore tool should ensure media reliability and reliability of online backups.

■ *Does the tool provide alternate backup server and tape device support?*

A failure on a backup server or tape device should cause an automatic switch to a different backup server or device.

■ *Does the tool restart failed backup and restore jobs for single and multiple jobs?*

A backup or restore job could fail midstream for any number of reasons. The backup tool should automatically restart the job from the point it left off.

Performance

The performance of the backup architecture is critical to its success and involves more than just the performance of the backup tool itself. For additional information on this topic, see Chapter 4, "Methodology: Planning a Backup Architecture" on page 61.

Ask the following questions:

- *Will the backup tool performance meet your requirements?*

    The efficiency of the backup tool—for example, the speed at which it sends data to the tape devices—varies from product to product.

- *Does the tool's restore performance meet your requirements?*

    The efficiency of the backup tool—for example, the speed at which it sends data to tape devices—varies from product to product.

- *Does the performance of a full system recovery meet Business Continuity Planning requirements?*

    If the tool will be used in disaster recovery procedures or business continuity planning, it must meet those BCP requirements. For example, many BCP requirements specify a maximum amount of time for the restore of all data files and rebuilding of any backup catalogs or indexes.

- *Does the tool provide multiplexed backup and restore?*

    To achieve optimum performance, the backup and restore tool should read and write multiple data streams to one or more tapes from one or more clients or servers in parallel. For additional information on multiplexing, see "Multiplexing" on page 22.

- *Does the tool enable control of network bandwidth usage?*

    The backup and restore tool should have the option of controlling network bandwidth usage.

- *Is raw backup support provided?*

    The backup and restore tool should be able to back up raw partitions. Under some conditions, raw backups can be faster than file system backups. (See "Physical and Logical Backups" on page 17.) Also, determine if an individual file can be restored from a raw backup. (See "Raw Backups With File-Level Restores" on page 24.)

- *Is database table-level backup support provided?*

    If in some situations individual tables in the environment could be backed up rather than backing up the entire database, the performance of the backup architecture could be significantly increased. The backup tool must support this option.

- *Does the tool provide incremental database backup?*

  This feature is important, since it is impractical to back up an entire database every hour. Incremental backups significantly increase the performance of the backup architecture.

Ease of Use

Ask the following questions:

- *Is it easy to install and configure the backup tool?*

  For a large corporation this issue may not be a major consideration, since it is possible to use the vendor's consulting services during product installation and configuration. For smaller organizations, ease of installation and configuration could be more important.

- *Does the tool provide backward compatibility?*

  Backup tool versions should be compatible with earlier versions of the tool. This makes it possible to recover data backed up with earlier versions of the tool. This also enables upgrading without the need to change the backup architecture.

- *Are error messages clear and concise?*

  If this is not the case, delays or difficulties could occur when attempting to recover data in an emergency situation.

- *Is message log categorization and identification provided?*

  This function will make it easier to diagnose problems.

- *Is the tool's documentation clear and complete?*

  Good documentation is fundamental to proficient use of the tool.

- *Does the tool's vendor provide training?*

  A training package should be included with the purchase of any backup tool. The vendor should be available to conduct on-site training of operations staff and to supply documentation about the specifics of your configuration.

- *Does the vendor provide worldwide customer support?*

  Technical support should be available around the clock from anywhere in the world.

Ease of Customization

The backup and restore architecture must be flexible and customizable if it is to serve the growing needs of a dynamic organization. Any efforts to design flexibility into the architecture can either be enhanced or limited by the backup tool chosen.

Ask the following questions:

- *Is it easy to customize the tool?*

  No two environments are the same. Highly customized backup and restore infrastructure may be needed to fully support business needs for a specific environment. It should be possible to modify the backup and restore tool to fit any requirements.

  For example, an environment may require a customized vaulting procedure. Or, an API may be needed that makes it possible to add and delete information from the file history database. This feature could be used to customize the backup and restore tool to interface with legacy disaster recovery scripts that need to be inserted into the file history database.

- *Does the tool provide state information from before and after a backup job is run*?

  This function provides the ability to place a wrapper around the backup tool. This is useful if a script needs to be executed before a database backup, for example, to shut down the database and perform related functions. Or, if after a full parallel export, to run another script to bring the database up.

- *Does the tool provide the ability to add and delete servers?*

  Hierarchical architecture enables servers to be added, deleted, and managed separately but still be encompassed into a single unified master management interface. The hierarchical design allows for easy scaling of the entire backup and restore infrastructure.

Compatibility With Platforms and Protocols

It is important that the backup tool supports the platforms and protocols specific to a business.

Ask the following questions:

- *Is the tool compatible with your past, present, and future operating systems?*

  Many different operating systems may need to be supported in a heterogeneous enterprise environment. These could include Solaris software, UNIX, Microsoft Windows, Novell NetWare, OS/2, NetApp, and others. The tool should back up and restore data from all these sources and should run on any server computer.

- *Does the tool support Network Data Management Protocol (NDMP)?*

  NDMP is a disk-to-tape backup protocol used to back up storage devices on a network. NDMP supports a serverless backup model, which makes it possible to dump data directly to tape without running a backup agent on the server. The backup tool should support NDMP if running small network appliances that do not have the resources to run backup agents. For further information on NDMP, go to

  http://www.ndmp.org

Compatibility With Business Processes and Requirements

The backup tool should support real business needs. These include the technology resources currently in place, as well as the day-to-day business processes within an organization.

Ask the following questions:

- *Does the tool support leading databases and applications?*

  The tool should support all leading databases and applications such as Oracle, Microsoft SQL Server, Sybase, Informix, Microsoft Exchange, and SAP R/3.

- *Are user-initiated backups and restores available?*

  In some environments, a backup policy may be in place to provide easy-to-use interfaces for end users—to reduce system administrator intervention. In other environments, user-initiated backups and restores may be prohibited. If user-oriented features are required, ensure the tool provides them.

- *Is vaulting support provided?*

  Vaulting can involve managing tapes, moving tapes out of libraries after backups are completed, processing tapes, and transporting them offsite to external disaster recovery facilities.

  For example, NetBackUp's BP Vault facility automates the logistics for offsite media management. Multiple retention periods can be set for duplicate tapes, which will enable greater flexibility of tape vaulting. BP Vault supports two types of tape duplication—tape images can be identical to the original backup, or they can be noninterleaved to speed up the recovery process for selected file restores.

- *Can data be restored in a flexible manner, consistent with business needs?*

  Depending on the different situations that arise from day to day, it may be necessary to restore different types of data, such as a single file, a complete directory, or an entire file system. The tool should make it easy to perform these kinds of operations.

- *Does the tool enable the exclusion of file systems?*

  There are situations when this feature is crucial, for example, when the Andrew File System (AFS) is used as a caching file system. To the operating system, AFS looks like a local file system. But AFS is actually in a network "cloud," similar to NFS. It may not be desirable to back up AFS partitions (or NFS partitions) that are mounted on an AFS or NFS client. For example, when backing up a desktop machine with different partitions mounted from other servers, you would not want to back up the other servers.

  With NFS, it is possible to tell when traversing into NFS space; however, AFS is seamless and therefore any file systems that don't need to be backed up should be excluded.

- *Does the tool support the security needs of a business?*

  The tool should support the security required by the operating system. If added data protection by encryption is required, the tool should support it.

- *Can jobs be prioritized according to business priorities?*

  Priorities for backups should be based on importance. For example, a critical database should take priority over less important desktop data.

- *Does the tool support localization?*

  The backup tool should provide the ability to run under a localized operating environment.

- *Does the tool support Hierarchical Storage Management (HSM)?*

  You should consider whether it is necessary for the tool to support HSM directly or integrate with an HSM solution?

Backup Catalog Features

The backup catalog lists historical backups, along with files and other forms of data that has been backed up. This feature of the backup catalog can be important to the performance and effectiveness of the architecture.

Ask the following questions:

- *Is an online catalog of backed up files provided?*

  A file history catalog that resides in a database will enable the user to report out of the database, perhaps using different types of tools. For example, the file history catalog may reside in an Oracle database. However, the user may want to report with different reporting tools such as e.Report from Actuate Corporation or Crystal Reports from Seagate. If the backup catalog resides in the database, the vendor should publish the data model. On the other hand, if the backup catalog resides in a flat file, no special database is required to read the catalog.

- *Does the tool provide the ability to quickly locate files in a backup database?*

  Tools that take a long time to quickly locate files or groups of files in the backup database can adversely affect recovery times.

- *Does the tool provide the ability to modify the backup database through an API?*

  If the backup catalog needs to be programmatically modified, an API published by the vendor should be used. If a standardized API is not available, it is not advisable to modify the backup database programmatically.

- *Does the tool provide historical views of backups?*

  It should be easy to determine which historical backups are available.

- *Does the tool provide a true image restore?*

  Restores should be able to recreate data based on current allocations, negating the recovery of obsolete data. (See "True Image Restore" on page 24)

- *Can the backup catalog be recovered quickly?*

  If a catastrophic failure occurs, the tool should allow the backup catalog to be quickly restored. The restoration can involve retrieving the catalog and indexes from multiple tapes.

Tape and Library Support

Ask the following questions:

- *Does the media (volume) database provide required features?*

  Indexing, tape labelling, customizing labels, creating tape libraries, initializing remote media, adding and deleting media to and from libraries, or using bar codes in the media database are functions that may be required. It is important to be able to integrate the file database with the media database. Additionally, the library will need to be partitioned, for example, to allocate slots in the library to certain hosts.

- *Is tape library sharing supported?*

  Tape robotic costs can be reduced by sharing tape libraries among multiple backup servers, including servers running different operating systems.

- *Is tape management support provided?*

  The backup tool should enable management of the entire tape life cycle.

- *Does the tool support your tape libraries?*

  Support should be provided for all leading robotic tape devices.

- *Does the tool support commonly used tape devices?*

  Support should be provided for all leading tape devices.

- *Can tape volumes, drives, and libraries be viewed?*

  The tool should report on tape usage, drive configuration, and so forth.

Cost

Backup and restore costs can be complex. Ask the following questions:

- *What are the software licensing costs?*

  Are software licensing costs based on number of clients, number of tape drives, number of servers, or the size of the robotics unit? These costs will impact the backup architecture and implementation details.

- *What are the hardware costs?*

  The architecture of a backup solution may require the purchase of additional tape drives, disks, or complete servers. Additionally, the backup architecture may require, or drive, changes to your network architecture.

- *What are the media costs?*

  Depending on backup requirements, media cost can vary considerably.

## CHAPTER 2

Backup and Restore Basics

This chapter provides an overview of concepts behind networked backup and restore technology.

Physical and Logical Backups

Physical backups copy a byte-for-byte image of an entire database, or raw disk partition to a backup device. *Logical backups* copy the logical entities in the database or the individual files in a file system to a backup device. Each type of backup presents a different configuration problem.

Physical backups are usually much faster than logical backups because the source is read sequentially and the data can be retrieved at full device speed. The drawback is that an entire raw partition must be backed up as a single entity. Therefore, physical backups are useful for backing up whole partitions. Physical backups require quiescent and internally consistent sources to ensure data integrity.

By contrast, a logical backup reads the logical entities, such as directory entries. These entries are read one at a time and are almost never in device order. While logical backups have lower throughput, they have the benefit of being able to inspect the last-modified date of each file and determine whether or not a file has been updated since the last backup. Logical backups can be faster than physical backups for performing incremental backups where relatively little data has been modified since the previous backup.

Logical backups also require some knowledge of the content and structure of the data being backed up. For example, a VxFS file system cannot be backed up with the ufsdump command.

Fully Consistent File System Dumps

Two different backup strategies are available when fully consistent file system dumps are required. One approach is to make the file system unavailable for modifications by unmounting it before dumping. The file system can then be remounted in read-only mode if read access is required while the backup is underway. The second approach is to lock the file system against modifications.

Because these methods prevent the file system from being modified during the backup process, they are usually implemented during off hours. However, if user batch jobs are also run during the backup process, their performance can be substantially degraded.

Full-Time Availability

Datacenters that require full-time availability of data can use software or hardware mirroring to replicate crucial data onto two or more separate disks or volumes. By itself, mirroring does not solve the real backup problem (nor do other protected storage mechanisms, such as RAID-5) because mirrored data is also susceptible to application bugs and user error. When full-time availability of file systems or databases is required, a number of options are available, including hot database backups, triple mirroring, and snapshot images (read-only copies of the data).

Database Backup Technology

There are three basic types of full database backups: online, offline, and raw device backups.

Online backups are logical backups of a database that can be run while the database is handling transactions.

Offline backups are logical backups of a database that is in a quiescent mode and is unavailable for transactions.

Raw device backups are physical backups of raw disk slices.

Online Database Backups

Using the online backup method is the least intrusive approach and is a popular solution for databases that must be available 24 hours a day. Online database backups can be achieved with software such as Oracle Recovery Manager (RMAN) or, on older versions of Oracle, with the Oracle Enterprise Backup Utility (EBU). These utilities can provide a consistent snapshot of all database table spaces to backup tools such as VERITAS NetBackup or Solstice Backup. With several parallel streams of data provided by the database, the backup tool uses the backup drives to their maximum capacity, multiplexing multiple streams into single devices where feasible. (For additional information, see "Multiplexing" on page 22.)

Since transactions must be logged during the backup process, database performance may be degraded when online backups are in progress. In very large backup situations, it is generally more cost-effective and faster to perform an initial backup to disk, and then roll the disk image off to tape. If a datafile, table, tablespace, or other entity becomes corrupted on the production mirrors, a copy is available and can be brought in relatively quickly. Although this method uses additional disk space, it completes faster than restores from tape.

Another method to accomplish online database backups is to use triple-mirroring. In this approach, a third mirror is synchronized to the other two mirrors sometime before the backup window begins. Once the data is synchronized, the database is made quiescent. An application, such as SAP R/3, is not brought down. The third mirror is broken, and the database is rolled forward. At this point, the third mirror is backed up to tape. When the backup is completed, the third mirror is logically reattached and resynchronized with the two-way mirror. This method of backing up allows for uninterrupted 24-hour processing while backups occur in a controlled manner. This method is currently used by several large Sun/SAP customers.

Offline Database Backups

For very large databases that can only be taken out of use for short periods of time, offline backups are often the best choice. Offline backups typically outperform online backups because of the lack of competition for system resources, and they have no impact on transaction rates once the database is back in use. Today, with high-performance backup tools such as NetBackup and Solstice Backup, offline backups can be considered a viable solution.

Raw Device Backups

Raw device backups are the simplest way to back up a database since they directly copy the raw disk devices to tape. The database has to be in an inactive state and requires the use of a tool such as NetBackup or Solstice Backup to manage the high-speed transfer of disk data to tape. Raw device backups can achieve high throughput because the database itself is not involved in the process, with all but essential overhead being eliminated. The disk devices are read sequentially, providing data to the backup tool at high speeds.

Advances in Backup Technology

In the past, IT organizations have turned to mainframes as a solution for high-speed backup of large databases. While UNIX systems typically delivered backup throughput of 50 to 70 Gbyte/hr, mainframes with their high-speed tape drives had a throughput nearly six times faster. However, several recent developments have turned the tables on this equation by enabling sustained backup rates of more than 1 Tbyte/hr on Sun servers while at the same time decreasing the intrusiveness of backup operations. Some of these recent developments are described in the following sections.

Faster Throughput Rates

Tape drive technology has seen dramatic improvements in throughput rates. The Mammoth 8 mm drive provides a native transfer rate of 12 Mbyte/sec with a compressed mode transfer rate of at least 30 Mbyte/sec. The STK 9840 drive, which competes with the IBM 3590 drive, provides a native transfer rate of 9 Mbyte/sec with a burst rate of 40 Mbyte/sec. A double-speed version of the STK 9840 drive is pending at the time of this writing. The DLT 7000 provides a native transfer rate of 5 Mbyte/sec. Linear Tape-Open (LTO) technology offers a native transfer rate of 12 to 15 Mbyte/sec.

Greater Capacities

Along with the improvements in speed have come improvements in capacity. The Mammoth2 native capacity is 60 Gbytes, with the compressed capacity typically being 150 Gbytes. The STK 9840 native capacity is 20 Gbytes. and the STK 9840 is designed to maximize time-to-data, rather than capacity. The Linear Tape-Open (LTO) and Super DLT (SDLT) technologies offer native capacities of 100 Gbytes, with even greater capacity for compressed data.

New Approaches to Online Backups With Database Technology

Recognizing the need for high-speed backups that require no downtime, database vendors have developed approaches to online backups that enable specialized backup software such as NetBackup or Solstice Backup to transfer data from the database management system (DBMS) to backup devices, using parallel streams of data. One example is the Oracle RMAN utility. This utility manages the creation of a database snapshot and feeds parallel data streams to the backup tool for multiplexing onto tape devices. Previously, this process required dumping database tables to separate ASCII files and then backing up the files. Today, however, RMAN provides a convenient API that can be used by third-party backup and restore utilities.

Automated Backup and Recovery Management Procedures

Another important development that is changing the character of backups is the advent of management software that automates backup policies and optimally feeds data to tape devices—ensuring integrity and the speeding up of the backup process. Raw tape speed and high-capacity drives are meaningless without the ability to effectively manage the transfer of data.

NetBackup and Solstice Backup offer built-in GUI-based schedulers. However, large organizations often use a third-party scheduler. A third-party scheduler takes advantage of the backup tool's command-line interface.

Some third-party schedulers:

- Control-M for Open Systems from New Dimensions Software
- Tivoli Workload Scheduler (formerly Maestro) from Tivoli Systems
- Tivoli Management Environment (TME) from Tivoli Systems

- Platinum AutoSys from Platinum Technology
- Event Control Server (Global ECS) from Vinzant

What are the tradeoffs between using a backup tool's built-in GUI scheduler and a third-party scheduler? A script-based approach with a third-party scheduler is more complex to implement but provides greater automation and power.

If a large number of backup jobs need to be automated or if other types of jobs (besides backup jobs) need to be automated, a third-party scheduler could be used. For example, one large organization backs up more than 10,000 machines each night.

Using a script-based approach with a third-party scheduler is safer than allowing an individual to manipulate the entire schedule with a GUI tool. Furthermore, if a script-based approach is used, the script can be regenerated on-the-fly each night, thereby performing a more sophisticated scheduling than could be accomplished using a GUI. For example, a query could be performed to determine which file systems exist and are mounted and then generate a script to backs up those file systems.

Another important point to consider is that third-party schedulers are event based and can schedule jobs and react to events that are outside the domain of the backup tool. For example, you might not want to run a backup job until a particular report has finished running or until a large database update job has completed. This choice is easier to accomplish with a third-party scheduler.

Multiplexing

Backup tools such as NetBackup and Solstice Backup now make it possible to run multiple backup jobs simultaneously and to stream data to one or more devices. This technique is known as multiplexing. Multiplexing can be accomplished in two ways:

- *Across tape devices*

   Multiplexing across tape devices allows high throughput to the tape subsystem.

- *Across input streams*

   Multiplexing input streams allows more data to be staged to tape, allowing full tape bandwidth use.

The streams can originate from locally attached disks or from clients over a network. As jobs finish, the backup tool can dynamically add more backup streams to the backup device. The configuration can be tuned to the desired level of multiplexing for each backup device. These backup tools also make it possible to initiate parallel restores from multiplexed images on tape.

Multiplexing makes it possible to keep a fast tape drive running continuously. Continuous operation is important for DLT drives since they require a relatively long time to spin up. The multiplexing needs to be set high enough on a tape drive so that it can accept enough streams to keep it continuously busy. In some situations, multiplexing might be set to just one stream. This can be the case when one or more tape devices connect directly to a large Oracle database. The tape devices can run at full speed in this scenario. In other situations, the multiplexing might be set to as many as 20 or 30 streams per tape drive.

For example, a nationwide car rental business backs up 1000 desktop machines from various airports in the country to a centralized location. Some streams come off 56 Kbit/sec leased lines, some come off 128 Kbit/sec ISDN lines. The data comes in from all over the country, so the multiplexing is set to 20 to 30 streams per tape. This practice ensures the tape drives are kept busy.

If multiplexed tapes need to be duplicated for offsite storage or other purposes, there are two options. Exact copies of the tapes can be created so that the copies contain the data in multiplexed format. Alternatively, the tapes can be demultiplexed on-the-fly during duplication. A demultiplexed tape can be restored more quickly. However, demultiplexing requires additional machine cycles. Usually, a dedicated backup server is used for this purpose. Typically, a higher priority will be placed on demultiplexing the most important datasets so these can be restored faster.

Compression

Data compression can be used to reduce tape storage requirements, improve backup speed, and possibly reduce network traffic. Two compression options are available: the software compression functions built into tools such as NetBackup and Solstice Backup, or the compression functions provided by dedicated hardware on tape drives.

It is better to use the hardware compression on tape drives if there is sufficient network bandwidth to support noncompressed network traffic. Hardware drivers offer higher performance, with compression comparable to software compression, however, hardware compression generally uses a device-specific format. The use of hardware compression reduces tape portability, since a tape may have to be read on the same type of device that originally wrote the compressed data. If data is compressed prior to being sent over a network, it occupies less bandwidth; however, the performance of the backup client will be degraded because the compression software requires CPU cycles.

For further information, see "Compression" on page 78 and "Data Type" on page 63.

Raw Backups With File-Level Restores

NetBackup now offers a feature, called VERITAS NetBackup FlashBackup, that improves backup performance in certain situations, although restores of files backed up in this way may be slower. FlashBackup performs a fast backup of an entire raw partition as it bypasses the file system. However, it does keeps track of the inode information so that individual files can be restored. This approach works well if a backup of a large number of small files is required. Furthermore, backup catalog sizes are smaller with this approach, since it is not necessary to keep all the file information in the backup catalog.

True Image Restore

NetBackup also provides a function called *true image restore*. This function can restore a file system to its most recent state. When this feature is enabled, additional information is collected during an incremental backup. NetBackup tracks any files that were added or deleted since the last backup. For example, an incremental backup was performed on Monday, Tuesday, and Wednesday. However, on Tuesday, 80 files were deleted. Additionally, the disk crashed on Thursday. With a true image restore, the deleted files aren't restored since they were no longer present when the most recent snapshot of the file system was taken. This could be important in some situations. For example, a user may have purposely deleted files to make room on a disk. A full restore of all files that had existed since Monday would amount to
3.5 Gbytes of data, but the disk may only have a capacity of 2 Gbytes.

Automatic Multistreaming

Another new performance feature available in NetBackup is *automatic multistreaming*. If a server is attached to several disk drives, you can specify that all local drives are to be backed up as separate streams. With this feature, the data can be streamed to multiple tape drives, or multiple streams can be sent to a single tape drive.

This feature automatically multistreams drives from a single NetBackup class. For example, if 10 local disk drives are attached to a server, the multistreaming feature can send 10 data streams to the tape drive (or drives) which will increase performance. Additionally, multistreaming can automatically restart any failed streams by using the *checkpoint restart* function. This is important if a large backup job is in progress and a part of the job fails because NetBackup can restart where the job left off and redo any failed streams.

Fine–grained control can be achieved by using the command that creates a new stream, which allows the user to specify groups of subdirectories and files as individual streams. By using this feature, you can make portions of a disk into backup streams instead of entire disks as is the case with the *all local drives* command.

When should entire disks be multistreamed, and when should the streams be defined in terms of specific subdirectories and files? An entire disk might be streamed if the disk contains many subdirectories, especially if subdirectories and files are added and deleted frequently, for example, a file system disk that contains many directories which are often modified. In this case, if directories are added or deleted, it is not necessary to remember to update the corresponding NetBackup class. On the other hand, finer-grained control can be achieved if there is one large subdirectory that is segmented. In this case, a backup of the individual subdirectories could increase performance.

## CHAPTER 3

Case Studies

This chapter contains case studies that we developed by interviewing the IT staff at major corporations that use Sun Enterprise servers to run their core datacenter applications. Although these companies are real, the case studies are done anonymously.

Case Study: A Transition to VERITAS NetBackup

This case study involves a company we will call TechEvolve Corp. (Any similarity between this fictitious name and the name of any real company is purely coincidental.) The case study provides a high-level view of a major project to transition the TechEvolve backup architecture to a scalable and globally manageable system built on top of NetBackup. The company's previous architecture was built around several off-the-shelf tools and home-grown tools. Now, TechEvolve is moving to the new unified architecture to achieve global scalability, centralized management, ease of use, and the flexibility to meet growth demands in a dynamic environment.

Company Overview

TechEvolve is a leading technology company with several datacenters around the world. They run their core business applications on about 40 Sun Enterprise class servers, including one Sun Enterprise 10000 (Starfire), four Sun Enterprise 6500s, six Sun Enterprise 5500s, and several Sun Enterprise 3000s or 3500s.

TechEvolve supports many 24x7 systems, notably for their manufacturing operations. IT must therefore provide continuous availability for these systems. To this end, their datacenters use two-node clusters, implemented with VERITAS products including VERITAS FirstWatch.

The Sun Enterprise servers run Oracle databases, applications that interface to Oracle databases, Web front ends, middle-tier servers, PeopleSoft (primarily to handle the financial systems), home-grown manufacturing systems, order management systems, financial systems, and HR applications. The Starfire machine is used primarily to run PeopleSoft for two of the company's business units.

Currently, TechEvolve is sharing systems across multiple business units. However, they plan to move the individual business units to their own segregated systems in the future.

The group that manages the Sun Enterprise servers is staffed by system administrators and is responsible for managing and maintaining the hardware resources as well as the low-level software resources up through the OS level. The corporate databases are managed by a separate DBA group. These two groups are responsible for defining company-wide standards and procedures, including the backup and restore architecture. A separate operations group is responsible for carrying out the day-to-day operations, including overseeing regularly scheduled backups and managing the tape libraries.

Success, Growth, and Scalability Issues

TechEvolve has grown rapidly into a large and successful worldwide operation. As a result, their backup and restore architecture, which served them well when they were a smaller company, has become inadequate. The old solution does not scale well and is unwieldy. To address this situation, the company is completely revamping their backup and restore architecture.

They started evaluating backup tools for the new architecture in March 1998. Their current goal is to have the new backup and restore architecture in place around the time this book goes to press.

The stated project goals in this timeframe are:

- To roll out the new backup tool, NetBackup
- To have a new tape library vendor in place
- To do some level of consolidation of their tape libraries and the systems supporting them
- To begin to implement tape SANs (storage area networks) for backup and restore purposes

TechEvolve has several compelling reasons for taking on this large rearchitecting project. The old backup and restore architecture consisted of five different tools—three home-grown tools and two off-the-shelf tools. As the company has grown, the IT staff has experienced a greater need to consolidate administrative control and to provide consistency in the backup and restore procedures. With the old architecture, whenever it was necessary to restore data, an operator had to know which tool was used to back up a particular piece of data. The operator had to use the corresponding restore procedure. This situation sometimes caused confusion and delays. Also, there was no single catalog that could be used to locate all data that had been backed up. With NetBackup, the company has a single backup catalog and a single centralized tool for restoring files and data.

The legacy backup architecture at TechEvolve contained the following components:

- A home-grown tool for database backups. This was a script-based tool that provided a menu system for performing hot backups of the company's mission-critical databases. This tool was developed over a six-year period. Many parts of the tool are being integrated into the new architecture.

- A second home-grown tool backed up file systems that reside on UNIX servers. It consisted of a wrapper around commands such as ufsdump and ufsrestore.

- A third home-grown tool was used to back up Windows NT desktops.

- An off-the-shelf tool was used to back up NetWare servers.

- Another off-the-shelf tool was used to back up NetApp servers.

The company built an extensive backup and restore architecture around these tools. As mentioned, however, this solution became unwieldy and failed to scale adequately.

The company also experienced historical problems with the vendors of the off-the-shelf tools. These problems revolved around software bugs and support issues. In addition, the vendor of one of their backup tools was in a somewhat shaky position financially. The tool in question provides a wrapper around whatever backup technology happens to reside on the server. Therefore, rather than place a backup client on any desktops or servers, the tool interfaces directly with native facilities such as ufsdump. The complexities of maintaining this type of architecture did not bode well for a vendor that appeared somewhat shaky. In addition, there was a time about two years ago when this tool was the number one cause of downtime for the company's Novell servers. It was actually crashing the servers.

This backup tool did successfully take TechEvolve from a $200 million company with about 200 desktops, all the way up to a $3 billion company with more than 3000 Solaris operating environment desktops and servers. However, "there's a point where its architecture falls apart" according to an enterprise systems manager.

The home-grown tools also had support and maintenance issues. For example, if changes were desired, it was not possible to simply purchase upgrades. TechEvolve does not have the staff to maintain these tools on a full-time basis, so they wanted to partner with a company that could do this for them. As with their off-the-shelf tools, the home-grown tool approach had been adequate when TechEvolve was a smaller company, since it enabled them to cobble together an acceptable backup and restore architecture with relatively little expense. But, as they grew, this architecture became "out of control," as one manager put it.

Choosing the New Backup Tool

TechEvolve decided to build their new backup and restore architecture around NetBackup. The next sections describe their reasons for choosing NetBackup.

Hierarchical Architecture

The NetBackup architecture is hierarchical, enabling many slave backup servers to be controlled by relatively few master backup servers. The master servers are rolled up to a single master-of-masters server that provides a centralized control point for managing the entire backup and restore infrastructure. This hierarchical architecture is important to TechEvolve because it enables them to easily add backup nodes as necessary to keep pace with the company's rapid growth. This architecture is also nicely suited to the organizational structure of TechEvolve, which maintains several datacenters on different continents. The company can locate master backup servers in these locales and control them from a single centralized console at their world headquarters.

Heterogeneous OS Support

The company supports a heterogeneous computing environment, and they needed a product that would support all of the following:

- Solaris Operating Environment
- Sun OS 4.x software
- Windows NT
- Windows 3.1
- Novell NetWare
- OS/2
- Network Appliance
- ClearCase (source code control system), which uses data files that need to be backed up in a very specific manner
- AFS (Andrew File System), which "is tricky to back up," as a company manager points out

NetBackup provides support for all of these environments.

Tape Library Support

NetBackup supports the tape libraries that the company currently uses, as well as the libraries that they plan to use in the future. These include ATL and StorageTek libraries.

API Available

NetBackup provides an API for controlling its functions programmatically. TechEvolve might use this API in the future to interface NetBackup with their home-grown backup tool for Windows NT desktops. The company has not decided whether this tool will be completely phased out or whether it will be integrated with NetBackup. If the decision is made to keep it, however, the NetBackup API can to integrate that tool into the overall architecture that they are building.

Support for NAS and Thin Servers

NetWare and Network Appliance, which manage network attached storage (NAS), are thin servers that cannot support a local backup client. Because of this, TechEvolve needed a backup tool that supports Network Data Management Protocol (NDMP). NDMP is currently the only way to back up an NAS server. TechEvolve has around 200 to 300 Gbytes of data for each of its NAS servers, so this was an important requirement.

Relationship With the Vendor

TechEvolve has an "excellent relationship" with VERITAS Software Corporation according to an enterprise systems manager. They use VERITAS file system products and high availability products. The company is happy with these products, and they have been successful for the company over the years. They like the support they have gotten from VERITAS with other products.

They consider VERITAS to be the UNIX leader for backup products. And since, at the time of this writing, VERITAS was in the process of acquiring Windows NT backup software vendor Seagate Software, TechEvolve felt this acquisition positions VERITAS to be at the top of the entire backup industry.

Complete Solution

TechEvolve wanted a product that could solve all of its backup needs, not just two or three. NetBackup could handle Oracle as well as Microsoft SQL Server databases. It could work over the network, as well as locally. It could perform backups in parallel or individually. The company came up with a test plan and then performed an evaluation. Ultimately, they made the determination to go with NetBackup.

Designing the New Architecture

The major thrusts of TechEvolve's new backup and restore initiative are to do the following:

- Evaluate and purchase enterprise class tape libraries.
- Rearchitect service levels with business units.
- Consolidate all five legacy backup tools into one consistent architecture under NetBackup.
- Move to tape SANs.
- Consolidate not only on the software side, but on the hardware side as well.

Choosing the New Tape Libraries

In their legacy backup and restore architecture, TechEvolve primarily used ATL tape libraries to handle backups. They have just over 30 P1000 class libraries, each of which supports 30 tape cartridges and 4 drives. They also have around 200 stand-alone DLT drives that are placed in many different locations around the world. Swapping tapes and managing libraries in an environment like this is a "complete nightmare," a manager said.

The company wanted to move to true enterprise class libraries. They wanted to have fewer tape libraries with a larger capacity of 10 to 16 drives per library. They evaluated both StorageTek and ATL and settled on StorageTek.

Here are the main criteria that they used to select a tape library vendor:

- *Reliability*—This was their number one issue. They actually brought vendors in to help evaluate their test plans.
- *Large-capacity libraries*—They wanted 10- to 16-drive libraries that hold a minimum of 400 tape cartridges.
- *Support for mixed media*—They are primarily using standard DLT tapes right now. However, in the future they want to be able to use DLT8000, DLT10000 (known as super DLT), and Linear Tape-Open (LTO) technology when it becomes available.

- *Hot-pluggable features*—They sought availability features, such as hot-pluggable power supplies and tape drives.

- *SAN support*—They needed fiber-optic technology support.

- *Solid company*—They wanted a vendor with a proven company track record and good OEM relationships with vendors that TechEvolve is currently using.

Ultimately, they will use about 10 to 12 of the larger StorageTek libraries to replace the 30 or so smaller libraries that made up their legacy architecture.

The main reason for this change is that it is easier to manage a few larger libraries. It is also cheaper and more efficient from a service and support standpoint. For example, larger libraries provide more hot-plug features.

Larger libraries are also easier to share among backup servers because of their higher speeds and greater capacities. For example, in the old architecture, the company did not share libraries between NetApp servers and other servers. Currently, they are still using dedicated NetApp libraries. But this will change as more of the larger libraries are brought online.

Architecting Service Levels With the Business Units

One of the major thrusts of this project was to rearchitect the service-level agreements between IT and the business units. The company undertook a process of reevaluating the processes and procedures behind the schedules, in terms of how long tapes are kept, how disaster recovery is handled, and so forth.

The old approach was to "back up everything and keep it forever." This was acceptable when TechEvolve was a 200 million dollar company. But they can no longer sustain this approach.

The company hired consultants to help evaluate their processes and determine how best to improve them. They looked at how to build better service-level agreements with the business units and how the policies will be implemented.

The IT team started by considering the data to be backed up. They needed to understand completely the data that exists and the criticality of that data. For example, a secretary's desktop data might not be as extensive or as critical as an engineering database.

Service levels are now defined largely around issues pertaining to the amount of data and the criticality of the data. To implement a service-level agreement, it is sometimes necessary to purchase new equipment. For example, if a large amount of data must be backed up within a fairly small time, such as three hours, it might be necessary to add CPUs to the server that will perform this backup operation or perhaps attach another tape device to that server. If the backup window could be extended to a 12-hour period, the additional hardware might not be necessary.

Implementing a service level can also affect the operational procedures that must be put in place. For example, if data is considered to be very critical, the business unit may want to duplicate the tapes at the back end and support more stringent vaulting procedures. Therefore, the amount of data can often affect purchasing plans for backup hardware and software. The criticality of that data often impacts the operational procedures that must be performed after the data is backed up, possibly affecting staffing requirements, offsite storage requirements, and so forth.

The TechEvolve staff has developed four service levels for their customers: gold, silver, bronze, and default. Each service level is associated with specific goals in terms of system availability, recovery time, level of DBA service, and so forth. The staff has developed reliability metrics that they can use to match their actual performance against their goals. This is how they are reviewed.

TechEvolve's gold manufacturing systems are slated to be available on a 24x7 basis, and the requirement is usually to have the database up and running within one hour of failure. Understandably, they might sometimes fall short of the one-hour recovery goal. But they must design their systems so that it is possible to recover from any type of failure that they can imagine within the hour. They have found that backing up to tape doesn't usually satisfy this requirement. So, they generally use a separate set of disks on the same machine and perform a hot backup of the database to those disks, creating a compressed image. Therefore, the option for quick recovery is to reconstruct a database from the compressed disk image. However, they also copy the compressed hot-backup image to tape by using NetBackup. This adds another level of protection, although they will not be able to restore within the desired timeframe if they are forced to recover from tape.

Within NetBackup, it is possible to use *classes* to define backup types, assign backup types to media pools, and so forth. The TechEvolve staff considers it important to use classes to implement different service levels. For example, gold machines are given dedicated tape backup devices through a NetBackup class. Silver machines can share tape backup devices with a few other machines. Bronze machines generally share tape backup devices with other machines in a pool of widely available devices. The class mechanism helps the staff to easily define service levels and to evolve those service levels in a flexible manner.

The service levels also define such things as:

- How long tapes are kept online—usually two weeks for gold systems, and one week for silver or bronze systems
- How long tapes are kept at the library
- How many copies of tapes are kept in libraries

The exact meaning of the different service levels (gold, silver, and so forth) is specific to the individual business units. For example, some business units require that highly critical tapes be duplicated and that some copies of the tapes be left in a library while other copies are vaulted. Other business units do not have this requirement because their business models are different. The associated costs often come into play when these kinds of choices are being made. TechEvolve's IT staff is glad to be in a position to offer this level of flexibility to their customers.

Integrating Oracle Into the Architecture

The integration points between the database and file system backup tool, in this case NetBackup, are always a tricky problem. TechEvolve needed to ask: How do we plug this technology into our infrastructure?

They ended up using a shell script wrapper to ensure paths and binaries are set correctly to invoke NetBackup. For example, NetBackup has a shared library called lib_obk.so which is used as the Oracle integration point.

In Oracle 7 the API is the Oracle Enterprise Backup Utility (EBU), and in Oracle 8 the API is the Oracle Recovery Manager (RMAN). NetBackup ties into both of these interfaces. There is also an older API, called Oracle Backup, that Oracle provides, but TechEvolve was not concerned about implementing it because all of the company's databases are currently at the EBU or RMAN level.

Scheduling Backup Jobs

Job scheduling is something the TechEvolve staff had to discuss and consider at length. NetBackup provides a user friendly GUI interface, but the TechEvolve team needs to coordinate backup jobs with other processes in their system. For example, there are times when they want to perform a backup immediately before or immediately after a large accounting batch job or manufacturing process.

To meet their scheduling needs, they looked for a third-party scheduler. The shell script wrapper that they use to invoke NetBackup turned out to be helpful because they can call it from any scheduler. Plus, that wrapper can be used if a DBA wants to fire off a job manually from a location where the GUI cannot be accessed.

The TechEvolve staff is still evaluating third-party schedulers at the time of this writing. They mostly use cron right now. They have an internally written process scheduler which they could easily hook into the new backup architecture, although they have not done that yet. They are also considering using the PeopleSoft process scheduler.

The basic default backup schedules consist of weekly full backups, with nightly incremental backups. Individual business units can modify this routine as desired. This is another example of how the use of NetBackup classes can be useful for defining service levels. For example, a bronze service level for one business unit can be defined to perform full backups weekly, while the bronze level for another business unit can perform monthly backups. The NetBackup class feature easily supports this type of flexibility.

Optimizing Recovery Time versus Backup Time

People on the TechEvolve staff mentioned that they consider it more important to optimize recovery time, rather than backup time. There is a tendency in the industry to focus on backup time, but TechEvolve would like to see more focus on recovery time.

In their service-level agreements with the different business units, IT agrees to a certain period of time that will be required to recover data in the case of a failure. This is often an hour or so for their larger systems. Restoring from tape is not always an option because of the time it takes to read a tape. In these cases, the range of solutions include backing up the data to disk, maintaining a standby machine, or even maintaining a complete failover site. While the TechEvolve staff universally praised NetBackup, they felt that if the tool placed more emphasis on recovery time, they might not have to implement some of these standby solutions and failover sites.

For example, the NetBackup catalog is currently a flat file. In a large organization, the backup catalog can reach hundreds of Mbytes in size. Members of TechEvolve staff have been working with VERITAS, suggesting that the backup catalog be implemented as a database. They believe VERITAS has been receptive, and they may proceed in that direction. (Note, however, that other people believe that there are advantages to keeping the NetBackup catalog as a flat file since, for example, it is possible to read a flat file with any editor.)

Architecting Tape Storage

To implement their backup and restore architecture, TechEvolve is currently using a combination of directly attached tape libraries and tape drives, along with networked backup servers. Systems that host more than about 20 Gbytes of data are backed up locally, not over the network. So, if a system hosts 20 Gbytes of data or more, they split out a tape drive from a library and directly connect it to that server.

This approach is expected to change significantly in the near term. TechEvolve is building a tape SAN and will back up their servers onto the SAN, rather than using directly attached tape devices. This approach will enable them to allocate tapes as needed to any server connected to the SAN. Ultimately, they will do away with directly attached tape devices altogether, since the servers will be "directly attached" to the SAN instead. However, they still plan to do normal network backups for servers that host less than 20 Gbytes of data.

Manual Backups versus Automatic Backups

The company minimizes the use of manual backups and does not make user-directed backups available at all. Therefore, any manual backups must be initiated by IT staff members, not end users. The company wants to automate the entire process because it is expensive to involve people in the backup process. It is also less efficient from a robotics standpoint. A manager points out that many companies, including TechEvolve, own a lot of stand-alone tape devices (in addition to their tape libraries). This is very inefficient and error prone because, for example, you need to have people swapping the tapes in and out of these drives. TechEvolve plans to eliminate all stand-alone tape drives as they move to a SAN-based architecture.

Note – Should You Move to a Tape SAN?

The decision to eliminate all stand-alone tape drives and move to a tape SAN is a site-specific decision and may not be the correct decision or best practice at all sites. You should examine all the advantages and disadvantages along with your company's business needs before making this decision.

Consider the following questions when making this decision:

Is tape SAN technology mature enough for a production environment? You will be using your backup architecture to ensure the safety and integrity of all of your company's business data. Whatever technology you choose must be stable enough to back up your data and restore the data. An accurate, consistent, and restorable backup is far more important than a fast backup that cannot be restored.

Are there hidden serviceability issues? Some software and hardware vendors provide enhancements, patches, and firmware updates on tape only. Do not eliminate all stand-alone and locally attached tape drives if you will be removing the only patch installation method your vendor provides.

What are the disaster recovery implications of a tape SAN? A separate, easy-to-restore backup of your system disk should regularly be created with ufsdump. You should not choose a tape SAN if it will negatively impact your ability to perform a complete OS recovery.

Designing the Master/Slave Hierarchy

The company's new architecture is based on NetBackup's master/slave hierarchical architecture, with a master-of-masters server, or *global data master*, located at their world headquarters. They are using the VERITAS Global Data Manager (GDM) utility to implement the global data master. A manager points out that many companies currently use only master/slave relationships in their systems. The GDM enables TechEvolve to implement an all-encompassing umbrella system where backup and recovery can be managed across all business units. At the same time, this architecture gives the individual business units the flexibility of having their own master servers.

At TechEvolve, each business unit now has its own top-level master server. The responsibility for managing that server falls on that particular business unit. This approach allows a great deal of flexibility in the services that IT can offer its customers. For example, IT can set up and maintain business-unit-specific backup schedules on the corresponding master server. But, GDM can still centrally manage the entire architecture, execute restore requests, set company-wide standards, and so forth.

Within the business units are a number of slave backup servers for each master server. Some slave servers perform network backups, and some perform locally attached backups. At the time of this writing, the locally attached backups are still being done via SCSI-connected tape devices. However, as mentioned previously, locally attached devices will soon be replaced by fiber-channel connections to a tape SAN.

Integrating UNIX and NT Servers

The backup and restore architecture used at TechEvolve makes little distinction between UNIX and NT servers. They share robotics devices across UNIX and NT servers. They do not differentiate backup types, classes, or service levels based on the server type (UNIX or NT). Rather, the differentiation is based on criteria such as criticality of the data, the needs of individual business units, and so forth.

VERITAS NetBackup FlashBackup

The company uses the VERITAS NetBackup FlashBackup feature in some situations. FlashBackup performs a very fast backup of an entire raw partition, bypassing the file system. However, it keeps track of the inode information so that individual files can be restored. At TechEvolve, they are using FlashBackup mainly in conjunction with their ClearCase source code control system. ClearCase uses a proprietary database and file system format that must be locked down before backups can be performed. The FlashBackup feature makes it possible to take a quick snapshot of the ClearCase database so that it can be brought back online as soon as possible.

TechEvolve finds that there is no need to use FlashBackup with Oracle databases, because Oracle provides the RMAN interface that TechEvolve uses extensively for hot database backups in their 24x7 environment. To obtain a coherent image of a database by using the raw dump obtained from FlashBackup, you must shut down the database before performing the backup (or in some other way obtain a static database image, such as splitting off a third mirror). TechEvolve does not have the option of shutting down their production business databases. ClearCase, however, does not provide a hot-backup feature such as RMAN, so ClearCase must be shut down to perform backups anyway. In this situation, FlashBackup provides the best means for the company to quickly take a snapshot and get ClearCase up and running again.

Multiplexing

TechEvolve is not currently using multiplexing. However, they plan to use multiplexing in the future. Multiplexing makes it possible to direct multiple streams of backup data from multiple servers to one backup tape drive, or from one server to multiple backup drives, or from multiple servers to multiple backup drives. (For more information see "Multiplexing" on page 22.)

One senior staff member expressed some concerns about multiplexing. He points out that when a single tape contains data from multiple data sources, the potential exists to lose data from multiple sources if there is a problem recovering the data from that tape. It is true that NetBackup provides the ability to copy a multiplexed tape to disk and then de-multiplex the data on that disk and back it up to multiple tapes. This approach is one way around the problem.

But TechEvolve probably is not going to take this approach. They do not plan to use multiplexing with their larger servers, but only with desktops that contain less critical data. After all, multiplexing is really a means of increasing the speed of networked backups. Since all servers at TechEvolve that contain more than 20 Gbytes of data are backed up locally (and will ultimately be backed up via a SAN rather than a normal network), only the smaller data sources would be potential targets for multiplexing anyway. By using multiplexing exclusively with less critical data, TechEvolve gets around the risk that a single point of failure (an individual tape) could cause widespread problems in recovering important data.

Server-Independent Restores

Server-independent restores is a feature of NetBackup that makes it possible to back up data from one server and restore the data to another server of the same type. TechEvolve uses server-independent restores in some situations. For example, if a server crashes and must be rebuilt, they may need to begin restoring the data before the server is completely rebuilt. With server-independent restores, one group can rebuild the server from a hardware and operating system standpoint while another group simultaneously restores the data to a different server. Later, the original server can be resynched.

Certain issues attend server-independent restores. One important issue comes up when a database has been corrupted. In this situation, you must restore everything you need with the database on the alternate server, not just the data that has been lost. Even with normal file system data, you must inform users that the data now resides in a different location. At TechEvolve, it is unusual to use server-independent restores with databases. It is more common for them to use server-independent restores with generic data that resides in a file system. For example, if an NFS file server goes down for several hours, system administrators can restore the file systems to an alternate server until the original file server is rebuilt.

Note – Server-Independent Restore Issues

The viability of server-independent restores depends upon the way in which the server is used. For example, a server-independent restore is usually not a viable methodology for a database server. Recovering a database requires more than just restoring the database itself.

The database software must be installed, licensed, and configured—then the database must be restored. In addition, device names may be different on the system where the database is restored. In this case, database system tables may need to be manually updated to reflect the differences in device names.

In contrast, a server-independent restore can be an excellent and efficient method to quickly restore the services provided by an NFS server. For the recovery of an NFS server, the exported (or shared) directories can be restored to any available system that supports the NFS protocol and has enough available disk space for the restored data. The name of the failed NFS server must be aliased to the alternate server in the name service until the failed server is repaired or rebuilt.

Whether server-independent restores are viable in your environment or not, they highlight a key point of any backup strategy: The operating system and data should not be intermingled. The operating system should be installed on a file system (or under certain circumstances, several file systems) and the application and user data should be stored on separate file systems or partitions, preferably on disks that are physically separate from the operating system.

This separation of operating system and data will make any type of restore easier to manage. In addition, this separation enables you to accurately tune your disk subsystem.

Planning for SAN

At the time of this writing, TechEvolve has not yet implemented a tape SAN architecture. However, they plan to use tape SANs with their backup and restore architecture. They expect to use StorageTek's Access Hub to allocate drives between units until they can use a switched fabric. Once switched fabrics becomes an option, they expect to use whatever switch and host bus adapter combination is recommended by the tape library vendor.

The lead architect mentioned several important design points for implementing a tape SAN. Bandwidth must be considered. It is important not to overload a fiber-channel loop by placing too many nodes on it. TechEvolve will probably use a small number of nodes, on the order of five or six. Each business unit will recommend how many nodes they want on their SAN. This is a function of how much data they need to back up and how fast their systems can push data over the fabric.

Database Backups: They Like It Hot (Sometimes)

A senior staff DBA at TechEvolve who has been around IT for 15 years says he feels this company has developed one of the best backup scenarios around. He has seen environments where backup and restore issues are taken lightly or somewhat seriously, but he feels that TechEvolve takes these issues very seriously. For example, he likes the way that they have prioritized recovery time over backup time. This is important in a high-transaction OLTP environment.

The senior DBA had only one small regret regarding the legacy database backup system: it was necessary to provide operators with DBA access to the corporate databases in order for them to do their work. The reason was that the scripts used by the operators required DBA access to perform hot backups. This meant that an operator had to regularly log in as a DBA. In the new architecture based on NetBackup, this is no longer the case.

The legacy scripts were combined into a menu-based internal application that they called BackupMain. This application was developed over a 6-year period. Not all of the work that has gone into BackupMain will be superseded by the new architecture, since the company can reuse much of the code in their NetBackup wrapper scripts and other places. However, much of the work has become irrelevant since many tasks are now handled by NetBackup.

The BackupMain scripts implement a simple menu-driven user interface for database operators. Not all of the features are pertinent to backup and restore operations. For example, BackupMain provides several database startup and shutdown procedures that the operators can use during off hours when no DBA is available. Therefore, someone without Oracle knowledge could shut down a database late at night. Much of this code will still be made available to the operators.

In addition, many of the company's database backup methods will be integrated into the new architecture. One of the interesting features of their system is that they rely not just on hot backups, as many companies do, but on database exports as well.

Two Backup Methods

TechEvolve performs database backups for two different purposes:

- *Database recovery* applies to situations where the database in general has been corrupted, perhaps due to a media failure such as a disk crash.

- *Data recovery* applies to a situation where data needs to be recovered, perhaps because someone accidentally deleted a large number of records or dropped a table.

For the purpose of database recovery, TechEvolve uses Oracle's standard hot-backup technology. The basic procedure is familiar to most DBAs:

1. Put the database into archive log mode. Doing so places the database data files into a consistent and static state, allowing them to be backed up. In the meantime, any transactions are pooled in the redo logs, so there is no interruption of service for the database users.

2. Use NetBackup to copy the data files to a compressed format on disk.

3. Re-enable the database, and run the redo logs to resynch the database.

4. Use NetBackup to back up the file systems (including the compressed database image) to tape.

Note – It is crucial that consistency checks be performed on the data at regular intervals and, if possible, before a backup is done. Consistency checks verify that the metadata has not been corrupted and may prevent you from backing up corrupted data. Furthermore, consistency checks may help you isolate corrupted data at an early stage. However, to perform a consistency check you may need to take the database offline or unmount the file system. For databases, the database vendor provides tools to perform these consistency checks. For file systems, the Solaris operating environment provides the `fsck` utility.

For the purpose of data recovery (and to provide an extra level of protection in general), TechEvolve uses Oracle's export utility to do the following:

1. Perform a nightly export of the database without taking it offline or placing it into any special mode.

2. Use NetBackup to back up the resulting flat file to tape. Note that this file may not be "read consistent" since database transactions may have occurred while the export was taking place.

The Oracle export utility drains data and all the structural definitions of the database into a flat file. That file could, in theory, be used to regenerate the database from scratch. Therefore, this procedure can serve as a last resort for reconstructing the entire database if the normal hot backup fails. But in this case, you would not get point-in-time recovery, since an export is simply a snapshot of the database and you cannot apply archive logs to it. Also, the reconstructed database might not be read consistent since transactions may have occurred during the export process. However, being able to recover data, even if it is not in a completely consistent state, is far better than losing the data altogether.

The main purpose of nightly exports in a 24x7 environment is for certain more limited data recovery scenarios. Suppose someone accidentally drops a table. This may affect only a few users. Perhaps it is localized to a portion of an application. In a case like this, it is highly undesirable to take the entire database offline and interrupt all users and applications. It may be far better to recover the data from the most recent export and perhaps reconstruct some of the data as necessary. The nightly export approach at least provides the option for localizing recovery operations when possible. This approach costs a little more from an infrastructure point of view, but once it is set up it doesn't really cost that much since the entire process can be automated.

Two Approaches to Backing Up Archive Logs

Oracle generates archive logs to track all transactions against the database, for the purpose of replay functionality. If it becomes necessary to restore a database from a hot backup that was generated a few days prior to a failure, all subsequent transaction logs can be replayed to bring the database up to the point where the database failed. This is accomplished by placing the database into *roll forward* mode, which reads the archive logs and reapplies the transactions. Every committed transaction is restored.

There are a couple of different approaches to backing up database archive logs. The particular approach that is chosen is mainly a matter of DBA preference. Both approaches are used at TechEvolve, depending on the situation and the service level desired by the business unit.

The two approaches are:

1. Back up archive logs as part of the normal hot-backup procedure for the entire database.

2. Back up archive logs as needed, separately from the hot backup of the database.

An advantage of the first approach is that all transaction logs are backed up at the same time as the rest of the database, therefore eliminating the need for separate backup runs. This approach can also result in faster restore times, since there are fewer archive logs to run to bring the database back to its most recent state. TechEvolve uses this approach mainly for smaller databases or databases that do not have high transaction rates.

The second option is usually better suited to larger databases or databases that have high transaction rates. If the file system that holds the transaction logs fills up, the database will freeze. To prevent this, TechEvolve uses a monitoring script that looks at how full the directory is and fires off a job to back up the archive logs once it reaches the 60 percent threshold. This job calls NetBackup which, in turn, calls Oracle. After the archive logs are backed up, they are automatically flushed out of the file system.

At TechEvolve the decision about which approach to use is related to service levels. For example, the gold service level performs separate archive log backups as needed. The company currently has around 200 to 300 corporate databases that they support in their centrally managed group. So, there are many different flavors and needs.

The backup strategy at TechEvolve requires a lot of tapes and is therefore expensive. (DLT tapes cost about $100 each.) The company uses two tapes for every archive log backup and approximately 15 tapes for hot backups of some of their larger databases. They could rearchitect their backup strategy to be less expensive, but this cost-saving could negatively impact the recovery side. As mentioned, their intention is to prioritize recovery time over backup time. As long as the time to back up doesn't interrupt processing, they would rather spend the money on that side than take the hit when a recovery comes around.

Note – Tradeoffs You Must Consider in Your Environment

TechEvolve has decided that the speed of data recovery is the most important factor in their backup architecture. A tradeoff like theirs is one of many that you will need to make when designing your backup architecture. Keep in mind that your business needs may determine or influence your technology choices. For example, your business needs may dictate that minimizing backup time and minimizing the implementation costs of a backup architecture are more important than minimizing recovery time.

Database Backup Schedules

At TechEvolve, hot database backups are performed nightly on all of the critical corporate databases. They do hot backups to disk and then roll the disk file systems off to tape, using NetBackup. Some of their databases are fairly large, in the 50-Gbyte range. They can use the disk backups to quickly restore a large database, which would take much longer to restore from tape. However, the tape backup is available as a safety net.

The hot backup to disk is exactly like the tape backups, except it is directed to a large file system on the database server. They also keep last week's copies of the archive logs to reduce time of recovery. This approach means that they are taking the hit on disk space, since the company must keep enough disk available to hold a compressed copy of the database.

Tradeoffs Related to the New Architecture

From the point of view of the DBA at TechEvolve, the new architecture primarily affects the backend processes, since NetBackup takes over where database backups leave off. However, there are many implications from the database end of things. Here are some of the tradeoffs that come with the new approach.

Archive Log Backups

The DBAs will have to manage their database archive log backups differently. In the old approach, database archive logs are backed up to two file systems. One file system collects the uncompressed archive logs. Meanwhile, a process occasionally drains the archive logs into a second file system where they are stored in a compressed format. The archive logs are then put out to tape in a compressed format. With the new architecture, NetBackup will pick up the uncompressed archive logs and perform its own tape compression.

TechEvolve liked the old approach of using two file systems, since it provides a buffer that helps to protect against the situation where the file system becomes full, leaving no room to store additional archive log data. This, in turn, causes the database to stall out. However, they can simply create a very large file system to keep the archive logs under the new architecture.

Less Customization of User Interfaces Is Available

The TechEvolve DBAs could more easily customize the user interfaces of the legacy tools. Since the NetBackup user interface is predetermined, they will no longer be able to do this. This capability is not considered very important, however.

Benefits Related to the New Architecture

Here are some of the benefits of the new architecture from the DBA point of view.

Less Manual Intervention

The operator no longer initiates backups. Any kind of job scheduler can call NetBackup. And, since NetBackup has a tape silo available to it, it can perform the tape mounting and handling automatically when it executes backups.

Easy Access to Backup Histories

NetBackup maintains a database of all backups. The database includes information about where those backups are located, what data they contain, what backups have been overwritten, what backups have been retained, and so forth. Because of this, the DBAs now have an online repository for accessing this type of information.

Recovery Is More Automated

On the recovery side, there is greater degree of automation. It is usually not necessary to ask an operator to mount a tape, since recently written tapes are kept in the libraries. The robotics can mount the tapes according to the database information. An operator can simply tell the system to restore certain data, and it does so across the network.

The newer versions of Oracle are getting better at providing utilities for automated recovery and building parallelism into recovery operations. But at this point, database recovery is still largely a manual operation. You must manually copy the files from tape back onto the system, verify that all files are present and in a consistent state, bring up the database manually, and then begin to roll the database forward. You must also make sure the archive log files are in a location where the database expects to find them. From this point on, the process simply rolls through the archive logs automatically, as long as all of the archive logs are available in sequential order.

The new NetBackup architecture does make this into a more automated process at TechEvolve, however. The new architecture enables a DBA to tell NetBackup the date of the database image to restore. NetBackup retrieves that image and brings it back onto the system. NetBackup locates the tapes and all of the associated archive logs and brings everything back onto the system.

Expected Reduction in Hardware Requirements

The new architecture will also reduce the amount of hardware that the company has to supply for many of their servers, especially when they introduce tape SANs to the system. There are up-front investments, but over time they should pay for themselves. For example, the company will not have to buy as much equipment to perform local backups. This approach may also free up I/O slots for disk controllers or other purposes.

Less Code to Write and Maintain

With the new architecture, DBAs do not have to write scripts to interface with RMAN, since NetBackup interfaces directly with RMAN. They will write some wrappers so that they can set up jobs in their job schedulers that can call NetBackup. This amounts to a more minimal level of programming on their side to write the wrapper scripts. The DBA staff will ultimately write a set of scripts that incorporate NetBackup syntax knowledge, since it is also necessary to perform manual backups at times. Therefore, if an operator needs to run an ad hoc backup job, the operator will have a script available to launch that job.

Case Study: A Solstice Backup Implementation

This case study involves a company that we will call LeadGlobe Corp. (Any similarity between this fictitious name and the name of any real company is purely coincidental.) This case study contrasts with the previous case study by providing a lower-level view of the day-to-day operations within a major datacenter, in this case, one that uses Solstice Backup (the Sun OEM version of Legato Networker).

Datacenter Overview

LeadGlobe has operations around the world, and their datacenters support operations 24 hours a day, 7 days a week, 365 days a year. The datacenters have grown and adopted new technologies along with the expansion of the company. Additionally, the volume of critical data, and services supported by the datacenter has increased.

Worldwide Operations

LeadGlobe maintains several large datacenters around the world. The datacenters run all core applications on Sun servers. The company supports a total of about 400 servers in their datacenters.

LeadGlobe transitioned from traditional mainframes to Sun servers in their datacenters because of the scalability and flexibility these servers offer. These features are a high priority since LeadGlobe is growing rapidly and must manage a massive order entry application. A LeadGlobe manager said it is difficult to tune and scale an order entry application in a dynamic environment using traditional mainframe technology. With client/server technology, the manager says, it is easier to add servers, storage, and databases to support load increases.

The scalability and flexibility of backup and restore operations is also greater within a client/server environment than within a traditional mainframe environment, according to the manager. The LeadGlobe datacenters include many servers that perform backups and many nodes that host data. These nodes include Solaris servers and applications. So, when new datacenter servers are added, the existing staff and backup servers are leveraged, possibly by adding more backup servers to the current environment. Therefore, the cost of maintaining the backup and restore infrastructure is reduced with the client/server architecture.

Also, the LeadGlobe manager points out, it is easier to make transitions to new technologies as they are introduced. For example, the transition from Mammoth tape drives to DLT tapes was easier because of the open systems architecture used within LeadGlobe.

Solstice Backup is the backup tool. The company's datacenters use a mix of applications on different servers, from clustered Sun Enterprise 4000 servers up to Sun Enterprise 10000 servers (Starfire).

Three Starfire servers are used for a major order entry application. Each Starfire is configured as follows:

- Four production domains, plus an additional spare domain
- 64 processors
- 7 Gbytes of main memory
- 300 Gbytes of disk arrays

Two Sun Enterprise 6000 servers are used in a Sun Cluster configuration. These servers support a data warehouse database.

LeadGlobe also uses about 40 Sun Enterprise 4000 servers in cluster configurations. Each cluster consists of two Sun Enterprise 4000 servers, with one disk array shared between the two servers.

The Sun StorEdge A5000 and Sun StorEdge A3000/A3500 disk array products are used. Storage area networks (SANs) are not used to attach tape drives at this time. However, the company is moving in that direction.

Major Datacenter Applications

The largest datacenter application at LeadGlobe is an order entry application, called ORD_FILL. This is a mission-critical application for the company, and it must be continuously available. A global shipment planning (GSP) application receives order information from ORD_FILL.

All applications are based on Oracle. The order entry system requires a large backend database of more than 150 Gbytes, which is hosted on a single Starfire domain.

Two front-end forms servers act as a launching pad for the application users. There can be 1000 or more users at any given time. Users log on to the front-end servers and do their job. The front-end applications access the back-end database, retrieve the data, and present the data to users by means of a GUI.

A single Starfire platform hosts this entire architecture by using different domains to support the front-end users, the back-end database, and the additional background processing that is required to run the system.

A second Starfire platform stands by as a failover machine. It is configured exactly like the primary Starfire server. Custom tools replicate the changes on the primary server to the standby server. In case of a failure or natural disaster, it is possible to simply switch over to the standby Starfire server and continue entering orders and performing all the tasks there were previously being done on the primary Starfire server.

A third Starfire platform is used as a staging server. This server is also configured identically to the primary Starfire server. A staging server is required because the LeadGlobe datacenter environment is dynamic, with many changes occurring at any given time. Application changes are tested on the staging server and then moved to the production servers.

The backup tool used is Solstice Backup, the Sun OEM version of Legato Networker. About two years prior to this writing, Solstice Backup was chosen. The effort was made to ensure that all the LeadGlobe datacenters supported the Solstice Backup product. Customized support tools were developed, including tools based on BMC PATROL and other third-party tools.

LeadGlobe Backup and Restore Architecture

LeadGlobe has transitioned from a centralized, mainframe environment to a distributed client/server environment. The backup and restore architecture has changed to reflect this transition, and to meet the increased data storage requirements.

Transition From a Mainframe Environment

A mainframe environment existed at LeadGlobe prior to October 1998. A major initiative had been put in place to switch to an open systems client/server architecture.

A recovery architecture team was put in place, using consultants from Oracle Consulting. IT staff at LeadGlobe represented the company's architectural standards in this team. Testing was done on Sun clusters and the Starfire server. The architected solution went live in October 1998.

Scripts automate several DBA processes that had previously been done manually. These scripts interact with Solstice Backup and store information in an Oracle database.

Tape Libraries

Exabyte tape libraries are used in the LeadGlobe backup and restore architecture. These libraries have a capacity of four tape drives per jukebox, where one tape can hold about 20 Gbytes of uncompressed data. In this configuration, LeadGlobe can keep up to 320 tapes available online. This amounts to an online storage capacity of 6.4 Tbytes of uncompressed data.

Backup Servers

Typically, a backup server consists of a Sun Enterprise 4000 that is directly attached to a tape library. Solstice Backup is the only software that is hosted on a backup server.

Storage Nodes and Private Subnets

Solstice Backup has a feature called Storage Nodes which allows a database server to act as a backup server. This feature makes it possible to back up data locally, without increasing the load on the network. This capability is an important consideration at LeadGlobe, since they must back up massive amounts of data every day. Unfortunately, the Storage Node feature of Solstice Backup was not yet available at the time LeadGlobe was implementing their backup architecture.

The company had to find another method to solve the network traffic problem. They ended up using private subnets between the database servers and the backup servers. Each database server has two network adapters, one that enables the users to connect with the database and one that is used solely to transfer data to the backup server. The company has load-balanced this scheme across the backup servers. They placed the Sun Enterprise 6000 servers used for the data warehouse applications on one backup subnet, and the Starfire server-based order entry application on a separate backup subnet. This approach has worked out well.

In the future, LeadGlobe will likely implement a storage area network (SAN) architecture that will replace the private subnet scheme and be used throughout the datacenters and the entire enterprise. The SAN architecture will make it possible to have a much more flexible system. For example, the backup planners will no longer have to be concerned about attaching libraries to specific servers on the basis of the amount of data that needs to be backed up on those servers. Instead, all backup data can simply be dumped onto the high-speed optical SAN network, which will copy the data to the available tape libraries.

SQL-BackTrack Fills Middleware Role

A product called SQL-BackTrack from BMC Software fills a vital role in the LeadGlobe backup and restore architecture. SQL-BackTrack runs on a database server. It extracts the database structural information and stores this information within a file system. For example, to perform a hot backup of the database, the SQL-BackTrack software compresses the data files and hands them over to Solstice Backup, which is used as a media manager for controlling the tape libraries. The tape libraries are controlled by a single server dedicated to Solstice Backup. This architecture is used in all LeadGlobe datacenters.

The LeadGlobe IT staff wrote scripts for automating the processes of installing and configuring SQL-BackTrack. Training was provided for the DBAs who became the production monitoring people.

Backup and Restore Processes

LeadGlobe has flexible backup and restore processes based on the service level required by the individual business units. These processes include schedules, tape rotations, various levels of backup, and offsite vaulting. As the size of the data has grown and service levels increase, the performance of the backup system has also been improved.

Backup Schedules and Tape Rotations

Full backups are applied to all critical databases at LeadGlobe every night. In addition, archive log backups are taken once per hour. Therefore, if a database crash occurs, the IT staff can restore the full backup from the previous night and apply each incremental archive log that has been generated since that full backup occurred. There is a tradeoff here in that the recovery time can be slowed by the potential need to apply many archive logs to roll forward the database. An alternative approach would be to perform full backups of the databases every four hours or every eight hours, but this would dramatically increase tape consumption and processor cycles used for backups.

The 80 online tapes are grouped into pools, and each pool is used for specific backup jobs. The daily backups are typically kept for four weeks. After four weeks, the tapes from the pool are recycled and rewritten during subsequent backup operations.

The month-end and quarter-end backups are typically retained for about 12 months. Year-end backups are retained for about seven years. To ensure that tape retention requirements are met, the tape libraries are preconfigured to retain tapes within specific pools for the appropriate length of time, given the purpose of those pools.

Note – Backup Media Shelf Life

It is important to consider the shelf life of your backup media when determining media retention schedules. For an eight millimeter tape cartridge, the maximum shelf life is seven years. In the case of LeadGlobe, this fits perfectly with their retention schedule. If LeadGlobe had a business need to retain their tapes longer, they would have required some other tape media, such as DLT.

Hot Backups, Cold Backups, and Mirrors

In the LeadGlobe datacenters, hot database backups are performed every day of the week except Friday. On Fridays, DBAs perform cold backups by taking the databases down and doing full backups. However, the critical highly available applications are never taken down. These include the order entry application that runs on Starfire servers and the data warehouse system that runs on Sun Enterprise 6000 servers. Only hot backups are used on these databases.

The feeling among some people at LeadGlobe is that cold backups are not really necessary; hot backups are always sufficient. But, the IT staff has instituted cold backups for those systems that can sustain downtime as a way to make everyone in the organization comfortable with the procedures that have been put in place. Some DBAs at the company simply feel more secure about the cold backup process, which completely takes down the database, flushes memory, and so forth.

Another approach would be to back up a highly available database by detaching and backing up a mirror, as described in "Online Database Backups" on page 19. However, this approach is not used at LeadGlobe. Some people at the company believe that this approach is too vulnerable to operator errors. For example, it is possible for an operator to detach the wrong volume. (Despite this, many companies do use this approach.)

Vaulting Procedures

Tapes are cloned every day at LeadGlobe, typically on the day following the backup. The cloned tapes are usually sent to an offsite vendor. This procedure is vital to the company's disaster recovery plans.

Vaulting support is provided in Solstice Backup. For example, a file system, such as /var, might be backed up onto a tape by a normal nightly backup. Then, Solstice Backup could clone the tapes used in the most recent backup operation. A cloned tape can then be kept in-house or stored offsite, using an outside vendor. Therefore, one tape remains online and can be easily used for normal restore operations. However, should it become necessary to perform a recovery with a vaulted tape, Solstice Backup can be queried for the clone tape number, and the outside vendor can be called so that the tape is retrieved and returned. For highly critical data, the service agreement with the outside vendor specifies that the tapes will be returned to the site within 1 1/2 hours. This varies, however, depending on the contract that is negotiated with the outside vendor.

The LeadGlobe IT staff appreciates the seamless way that Solstice Backup can access a clone tape in the case that the original tape is unavailable or corrupted. By simply removing the primary backup tape from the library and replacing it with the clone (which may have been retrieved from an offsite vendor), Solstice Backup knows to use the cloned tape without prompting from the operator. This is a feature LeadGlobe tested and found to work successfully. This feature makes recovery easier.

Note – Tape Cloning Considerations

If your backup architecture requires tape cloning, consider that when you choose a backup tool. Not only should the tool support tape cloning, but the tool should provide a mechanism (such as checksumming) to verify that the cloned tape is a complete and accurate copy.

Multiplexing

LeadGlobe uses the multiplexing feature of Solstice Backup. UNIX file system backups and database backups are often directed to the same tape. In addition, database backups are done in parallel. The database content is stored in a number of data files, and LeadGlobe typically sends two or three data files simultaneously to the same tape.

SQL-BackTrack is used in this process. It is possible to set up a certain number of parallel backup sessions when SQL-BackTrack is configured for the database. The rule of thumb at LeadGlobe is to configure the number of SQL-BackTrack parallel streams to be 50 percent of the number of data files. In a large database, there might be 40 data files. In this case, LeadGlobe would configure 20 parallel sessions. Therefore, when a backup session is started, SQL-BackTrack attempts to spawn the maximum number of parallel backup sessions, 20 in this case.

At the back end, the Media Manager component of Solstice Backup manages a given number of backup sessions per tape. The back-end configuration is done completely outside the context of the type of backups or the source of the backup streams. For example, eight parallel sessions are typically specified per tape, with four tapes per library active at any time. This amounts to 32 parallel streams per library that could be active simultaneously. These streams might consist of data from file systems or databases. The number of parallel streams on the back end is determined by the capacity of the tape libraries and tape drives, not by any considerations relating to the sources of the data (such as the number of data files in a given database).

Example Backup Architecture

The LeadGlobe backup architecture serves as an example of best practices at work. The next few sections provide a concise, detailed, and low-level view of the architecture. These sections are intended to be instructive by example.

Backup Components

The following software components are backed up daily:

- Oracle 7.3.3 software
- Oracle application files
- UNIX file systems
- Oracle database files
- Transaction logs/archive logs
- Logs and output reports

Software

The following software applications and instructions implement the backup strategy:

- *Solstice Backup v5.0.1a—* Solstice Backup media management software is installed on the Solstice Backup (SBU) server.

- *Open Backup Stream Interface (OBSI) Networker v2.1.2*—OBSI Networker integrates Oracle database backups with the Networker backup. The OBSI Networker is installed on all LeadGlobe datacenter servers.

- *BMC SQL-BackTrack for Oracle v2.3.0.5*—SQL-BackTrack is a backup and recovery management tool. The SQL-BackTrack software is installed on the primary (OLTP/ORD_FILL) server, the standby (ORD_FILL/REPLICA) server, and the data warehouse server.

- *AutoSys v3.3.7*—AutoSys schedules database and UFS backups.

Hardware

The backup hardware consists of a Sun Enterprise 4000 server with four Exabyte Mammoth 480 tape drives. Each Exabyte Mammoth 480 tape drive hosts eight magazines. Each magazine contains 10 tape cartridges. This architecture provides a backup capacity of 20 Gbytes of uncompressed data per tape, for a total of 6400 Gbytes of uncompressed storage. It provides a backup throughput of approximately 42 Gbyte/hr, using all four drives.

Supported Servers

The LeadGlobe datacenter backup system supports the following servers:

- *Primary Server*—The primary server is a Sun Enterprise 10000, with two Exabyte Mammoth 480 tape drives attached.

- *Standby Server*—The standby server is a Sun Enterprise 10000, with two Exabyte Mammoth 480 tape drives attached.

- *Data Warehouse Server*—The data warehouse server is a Sun Enterprise 6000, with two Exabyte Mammoth 480 tape drives attached.

- *Other LeadGlobe Datacenter Systems*—Other systems use the Sun Enterprise 4000 with Exabyte Mammoth 480 tape drives attached, and an Ultra 2.

Support Applications

The backup and restore architecture supports the following applications:

- ORD_FILL
- ORD_FILL-JRF/Replica
- FMR Data Warehouse
- ORD_FILL IH client
- ORD_FILL Red Pepper
- AutoSys
- RSYS/Error Management/System Operations
- GEM IH client
- GEM
- Red Pepper
- GSP US EDI
- GSP US
- GSP US IH client
- ProductShip
- GSM US EDI

Example Backup Types and Backup Frequencies

The LeadGlobe datacenter recovery strategy includes the following four backup types:

- Database backups
- Archive log backups
- SQL-BackTrack profile backups
- UNIX File System backups

The following sections contain a brief description of each backup type.

Database Backups

For fast and complete recovery, a full database backup is performed at least once a day. Since the database must be available on a 24x7 basis, a hot (online) backup of the database is performed nightly.

Before patches are installed or structural changes are applied to the database, the database libraries are backed up and a cold backup of the entire database is taken. Since these changes are required infrequently, this model results in maximum uptime for the database.

Archive Log Backups

For complete recovery from any failure, it is necessary to have a backup of all archive logs. Hourly backups of all archive logs are performed to reduce the risk of media failure. To expedite recovery, all copies of the latest archive logs are kept on a disk (in an alternate location) for a minimum of two days.

The arch_mgmt.sh script is used to accomplish these tasks. This script also helps with space management of the archive logs destination.

SQL-BackTrack Profile Backups

A SQL-BackTrack profile records the database's backup history and tracks the backup media automatically. Recovery is not possible without this file. This file is backed up along with database files during database and archive log backups. It is backed up onto the same tapes as the database files.

File System Backups

All file systems—including all application code and configuration files—are backed up once per day.

TABLE 3-1 shows the database status (up or down), the files that are backed up, and the frequency of backups for an Oracle server.

TABLE 3-1   File System Backups

Data Type	DB Status	Files Backed Up	Frequency
Offline full database (cold)	Down	Data files Control files Archive logs Parameter file BKTRK profile	Once a week
Online full database (hot)	Up	Data files Control files Archive logs Parameter file BKTRK profile	Once a day during off-peak hours
Archive logs	Up	Archive logs BKTRK profile	Hourly
UFS	N/A	File system Application code Configuration files	Once a day during off-peak hours

Secondary Backup Mechanisms

If an emergency prevents the use of SQL-BackTrack, other backup strategies are used.

- Raw partitions are backed up directly to tape through Solstice Backup by rawasm.
- Home-grown scripts use the dd command to copy raw partitions to a file system. After the scripts back up the raw partitions, Solstice Backup can copy the resulting files to tape.

Example Backup Schedule

This section presents the LeadGlobe backup schedule in TABLE 3-2. The actual database backup times are determined by the LeadGlobe IT staff, with input from the DBAs.

TABLE 3-2   Example Backup Schedule

Application	Sun Server	Database Size (Gbytes)	Backup	Frequency	Storage
ORD_FILL	Enterprise 10000	100	Hot Archive logs UFS	Daily Hourly Daily	Local
ORD_FILL IH client	Enterprise 4000	N/A	UFS	Daily	Central
GBM Red Pepper	Enterprise 4000	N/A	UFS	Daily	Central
ORD_FILL-JRF/ Replica	Enterprise 10000	100	UFS	Daily	Local
FMR Data Warehouse	Enterprise 6000	500	Hot Cold Archive logs UFS	Daily Weekly Hourly Daily	Local
AutoSys	Enterprise 4000	N/A	UFS	Daily	Central
Rsys/Error-Mgmt/SysOps	Enterprise 4000	N/A	Hot (Rsys) Cold (Rsys) Archive logs UFS	Daily Weekly Hourly Daily	Central
GEM IH client	Ultra 2	N/A	UFS	Daily	Central
GEM	Enterprise 4000	N/A	N/A	Daily	Central
Red Pepper	Enterprise 4000	N/A	Hot Cold Archive logs UFS	Daily Weekly Hourly Daily	Central
GSP US EDI	Ultra2	N/A	UFS	Daily	Central
GSP US	Enterprise 4000	N/A	Hot Cold Archive logs UFS	Daily Weekly Hourly Daily	Central
GSP US IH client	Ultra 2	N/A	UFS	Daily	Central
GSM US EDI	Ultra 2	N/A	UFS	Daily	Central

Example of Backup Architecture Map

FIGURE 3-1 maps out the backup architecture used in the LeadGlobe datacenter:

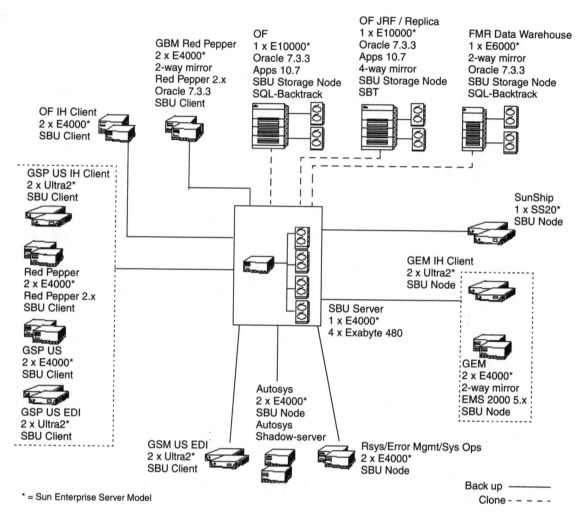

FIGURE 3-1   Example Backup Architecture

## CHAPTER 4

Methodology: Planning a Backup Architecture

The case studies in the previous chapter provided an insight into some best practices associated with backup architecture planning. This chapter outlines a formalized approach that can be used as a guide to plan a scalable backup architecture in a networked organization.

Capacity Planning

Capacity planning is an important component of a successful scalable backup architecture. Numerous variables and configuration permutations must be accounted for. Frequently, systems cannot do the required job because they use the wrong product. Installation and configuration can be complex, with many opportunities for error.

Within any system there can be interrelated bottlenecks; therefore, an important part of successful capacity planning involves minimizing the impact of any bottlenecks.

A capacity planner may be responsible for selecting hardware and software that will support efficient backup and restore operations in the datacenter and throughout the enterprise.

The first consideration in capacity planning for backup and restore architecture is the volume of data. In the management of this data, attention should be paid to the following:

- Availability of the data
- How data will be spread out across the network
- Policies for backing up the data
- Recovery requirements

The second consideration should be the backup server requirements:

- Network
- Storage
- Backup devices

Finally, configuration requirements should be determined.

Environment Considerations

The environment to be backed up requires careful analysis. This section provides guidelines for issues that require consideration.

Dataset Size

The first step is to determine how much data needs backing up or archiving regularly. Two main factors are:

- Total dataset size
- Characterization of dataset changes—how much data will be saved by the incremental backups

Total Dataset Size

The total size of the existing dataset is an indication of the minimum storage capacity required. The size of the dataset is the amount of data that must be backed up during a full backup and is the starting point in calculating the total storage capacity required.

Total dataset size can be one of the easiest pieces of information to obtain. In addition to determining total dataset size, the following information should be known or estimated:

- *Number of separate files*. The total volume of data may be composed of a few large files or millions of small files. Certain types of data, for example, databases, may not reside in files at all, but could be built on top of raw volumes. When a file system is backed up, there is often a small fixed overhead per file.

  Knowing the number of files helps determine the size of the backup catalog database. NetBackup product guidelines suggest allowing an average of 150 bytes in the database per file revision retained on the media. This works out to a gigabyte of backup catalog database for approximately seven million file records.

- *Average file size.* By knowing the total dataset size and the number of separate files, you can calculate the average file size for the environment. However, if there is a large skew in file size distribution, for example, many small files and a few very large files, this average may not be a good predictor of behavior. In this case, plan for different performance characteristics when backing up small files versus large files.

Size of Changes to the Dataset

The size of changes to the dataset determines the volume of data needed to be saved during incremental backups. The following should be known or estimated:

- *Frequency of dataset change.* The frequency of dataset change determines the frequency with which backups should be performed. This factor can vary widely. For example, some directories never change, some change only when products are upgraded, some change only at the end of the month, and some—like user mailboxes—may change minute-by-minute. The frequency of dataset change helps determine the volume of data written during an incremental backup.

- *Amount of data to be backed up.* A decision has to be made whether to back up all the data or only the changed portions. Although it is faster to save only changed portions, when it comes to restoring the data, it is usually faster to restore entire directories and file systems from full backups. This is due to the nature of the restore process. Restores that use incremental backups are first required to restore from the previous full backup and then apply all subsequent incremental backups. This multistep process can result in numerous tape mount requests. Also, the same piece of data may be retrieved multiple times.

The choice between full and incremental backups becomes a matter of priorities. Is it more important for scheduled backups to finish quickly? Or is the ability to restore data quickly more important? Restores are often subject to critical time constraints. Whichever backup type is selected, it should be performed frequently.

Data Type

The level of compression that backup hardware or software can achieve depends on the type of data to be backed up. However, there is no guarantee that similar types of data (to be compressed) will exhibit similar properties. It would be safest to assume the data is not compressed and to compress all data to be backed up.

Data from databases or high-level applications requires special attention for effective capacity planning. Unless the enterprise has simple data availability requirements, the backup infrastructure will require modules to save data from the application in a consistent state. These modules ensure correct restores and are available for many popular database and application environments, including NetBackup and Solstice Backup.

Consider the compression possibilities for these data types:

- *Text or natural language.* Text or natural language has a lot of redundancy and can be compressed effectively by both software and hardware technologies. For example, in tests using sample English texts, the DLT7000 tape drive hardware compressed the data at a ratio of approximately 1.4:1.

- *Databases and high-level applications.* Many popular database packages and application environments have corresponding backup modules for NetBackup and Solstice Backup. For example, backup modules are available for Oracle, Informix, Sybase, and for application environments such as SAP. These modules back up and restore data in a consistent state without taking the database offline.

  Additionally, databases and high-level applications commonly have varying structure and contents and often contain text or numeric data with large amounts of redundancy. These factors improve the effectiveness of compression. For example, in tests with sample databases from a TPC-C benchmark, the DLT7000 tape drive hardware compressed this type of data at a ratio of approximately 1.6:1.

- *Graphics.* Many applications manipulate numerous large graphical objects. The fact that graphic files are commonly larger than text files does not imply the file system will consist of a few large files, because applications create composite objects from a myriad of smaller isolated objects.

  In general, graphic objects are stored in a compressed state, making it unlikely that they can be further compressed by either hardware or software technologies. It has been found that hardware compression algorithms often inflate files already optimally compressed. For example, in tests with Motion JPG data, the DLT7000 tape drive hardware demonstrated a compression ratio of approximately 0.93:1.

- *Combined file types.* Data residing on network file servers and internet servers is usually a mix of text, graphics, and binary files. Because these datasets commonly consist of many small files, system performance must be closely analyzed. These mixed file types compress well. For example, in tests with files from network file servers and internet servers, the DLT7000 tape drive hardware demonstrated a compression ratio of approximately 1.6:1.

File Structure

Another factor that must be considered is the structure of the files. Will files be backed up by means of a file system or dumped from a raw device?

Raw dumps copy all the bits from the storage volume to the backup media. This process captures the bits for any file system or database metadata as well as actual application data written on the volume. However, the metadata may be out of synch with the data in the volume. This is because the metadata is not interpreted, and the volume cannot differentiate the backup from a different data access. To prevent this problem, the volume is commonly taken offline to prevent updates to both data and metadata. Another solution is to mark all entities on the volume as read-only for the duration of the backup.

The level of this problem depends on the type of file system and database to be backed up. Some high-level applications may keep their data and metadata within the file system, which requires the volume be taken offline or otherwise prevented from updating files during the backup process. It is mandatory to prevent file updates during backups so that all application data can be saved and restored in a consistent state.

The advantage of raw volume dumps is the efficiency of dumping or restoring raw data without further interpretation. Disk access is frequently large and sequential, minimizing the overhead of system calls and eliminating seeks.

Another consideration of raw volume and file system backups is the granularity of the data. A raw volume is treated as one large entity. With raw volumes, the entire dataset needs to be restored to recover just one portion of the data, for example, a file or database row. Incremental backups are currently impossible with raw volumes. Restoring an entire dataset not only takes longer, it also overwrites changes to data that had been made since the last dump. However, if a volume contains relatively little data, a file system dump could be more efficient than a raw volume dump, since a raw volume dump backs up an entire volume, whereas a file system dump just backs up valid data. Characterization of data use is important for determining whether to use raw or file-system-level dumps. For example, a raw dump of a 9-Gbyte volume that contains only 200 Mbytes of files is inefficient.

By contrast, file systems add additional overhead. Each directory is stored as a file containing the location of files in the directory. Files may not be contiguously written onto the disk. Reading the files and directories may require large, random seeks to locate the various parts of the files, which can reduce the effective data transfer rate from the disk volume.

File systems also have a number of features that can benefit from effective backup configuration and planning. Chief among these is the ability to use Direct I/O, which is a method of accessing files in the file system without using the virtual memory buffer cache. Using Direct I/O can result in large savings of CPU time and memory usage. However, despite the benefits of Direct I/O, the disk head still has to find the start of a file, which may require a long seek. A recent study demonstrated that, on average, Direct I/O saved approximately 20 percent on CPU cycles. By not using the buffer cache, the system can avoid memory contention between the file buffer cache and applications.

Direct I/O has been available in both the VERITAS File System (VxFS) and UFS since version 2.6 of the Solaris operating environment. VxFS provides numerous ways of engaging Direct I/O, including a per-I/O option. A common method of enabling this feature for an entire file system is to use a mount-time option. UFS also allows Direct I/O to be enabled for the entire file system. An additional benefit of VxFS is the way you can use different options to remount a file system without first having to unmount the file system. This feature allows users to remain online and active while Direct I/O is toggled, which can be important in situations where continuous operation is required.

The VxFS file system also provides a quick snapshot capability that can mount an additional file system as a read-only snapshot of the original. This is done while the original is still active and available. This feature is implemented by a copy-on-write mechanism which ensures that any block from the original file system is copied to a special area before the block is changed on disk. A relatively small amount of additional disk space is required to activate the file system snapshot capability since only blocks that change during the snapshot need to be duplicated.

Data Origin

Knowing where data originates can help you plan an appropriate configuration. The configuration needed for a local backup at high speed is different from the configuration needed to back up hundreds of small desktop systems over a metropolitan area network. Ask the following questions:

- *Does data reside on a server that performs the backup?*

  When data resides on a server that performs the backup, the complication of configuring the network is eliminated. The planning can be focused on the disk and tape subsystems and server processing capabilities. The server needs sufficient tape bandwidth to meet the backup window requirements (the available time period for backing up a specified amount of data). To ensure sufficient capacity for multiple backups—including daily differential, weekly cumulative, and full monthly backups—tape capacity should be configured to be from three to five times the dataset size.

  Disk bandwidth should be configured to meet backup window requirements and to keep tapes streaming. For example, the DLT7000 tape drive must receive data at a rate of not less than 3.5 Mbyte/sec in order to prevent back-hitching. (Back-hitching occurs when the flow of data to a tape is interrupted and the drive must stop and reposition the tape. Back-hitching consumes time, accelerates media wear, and reduces the mechanism life.) It may be difficult to ensure data is received at the correct rate because the server and disk subsystem are often already in place and tuned to a specific set of tasks. In this case, it can help to measure the sequential rate of the disk subsystem to determine if the desired backup window is feasible before planning for a specific set of tape devices. If the backup window is feasible but backup performance suffers because of slow disks, the disk subsystem may need to be reconfigured or upgraded as part of the system upgrade path.

You also need to determine whether CPU resources necessary to perform backups are available. For example, with Direct I/O enabled, a single 250 MHz CPU should be sufficient to perform backups at 50 Mbyte/sec from local disk to tape. If backups are concurrent with regular operations and the system is fully loaded, then additional CPU resources may be needed.

Other factors must be considered. Does the system have spare processing capacity? Determine how much head-room exists and whether it is sufficient to meet demands. If a backup is to be performed during off-peak hours, determine whether any other scheduled processes will run concurrently with the backup. If other process will be running, sufficient CPU resources should be available for all processes to run concurrently.

■ *Does data reside on remote clients?*

If the data to be backed up resides on remote clients, take into account their requirements. This can involve planning for a network configuration that meets the backup window requirements. There is no simple method for this since enterprise networks can be configured in numerous ways. However, for successful planning of network backup infrastructure, a sound knowledge of network performance is a must.

New storage devices may be added relatively easily; however, adding network capacity may require reconfiguring parts of the enterprise network. Infrastructure modifications at this level can be extensive and usually require advance planning. Therefore, even if an infrastructure upgrade is planned, there is often a period of time where the backup solution must work around inadequate network bandwidth.

Because of network bandwidth issues, a frequent challenge is to find ways to meet backup requirements within the restraints of a network bottleneck. To understand the overall situation and to apply an optimal solution, ask the following questions:

■ *How many clients are there?*

Knowing the number of clients helps determine the overall scale of the enterprise. It also helps to quantify characteristics of the backup architecture, for example, knowing the optimal level of multiplexing. A knowledge of client numbers can assist in determining the relationship between clients and their location to the backup server.

■ *What types of clients are there?*

To understand client processing requirements, you need to know the types of clients, their architecture, and which operating systems are being run. For example, if a client supports a powerful processing capability but network bandwidth between the client and backup server is constrained, some form of software compression should be used. NetBackup and Solstice Backup offer client-side modules for most platforms.

■ *Are clients connected to their own backup devices?*

If clients use a local backup device, the best configuration may be a hierarchical master-slave configuration. In this configuration, the master server initiates and tracks backups; however, the data is dumped to a local device. This configuration can reduce network traffic and significantly increase overall performance of the backup infrastructure. A master-slave configuration is recommended for large clients connected to a backup server via a slow network. The backup server is often not as powerful as the client it controls. The main backup devices are attached to the slave clients.

■ *How are clients distributed?*

Knowing where clients reside on the network can assist in determining the available network bandwidth between client and server. This information is needed to accurately predict backup times and data transfer rates. Because network bandwidth is often inadequate, a hybrid configuration, where some clients are backed up directly over the network and others are backed up locally within a master-slave configuration, could be a solution.

■ *How autonomous are client systems?*

Sometimes client systems are located in remote locations, connected to the backup server by a wide area network (WAN). Often these systems do not have a dedicated local administrator and therefore need to be managed remotely. A backup tool simplifies the process of centralizing management; however, some tasks still require manual intervention, for example, changing the tape on a stand-alone drive at a remote site.

■ *What does the disk subsystem look like?*

For maximum performance when modern tape backup technologies are used, the disk subsystem must be configured optimally. The reason is that disk access usually becomes the bottleneck (assuming network bandwidth is sufficient or backups are performed locally). The performance of disk subsystems depends on numerous factors. To evaluate disk-related performance issues, ask the following questions:

■ *How is data laid out on the disks?*

The data layout on the disk affects the throughput rate because it determines whether access to the disk is sequential or random. If the access pattern requires frequent seeks between portions of the disk, overall throughput rates will decrease dramatically. An access pattern can require frequent seeks for three principal reasons.

The most common reason is that data on the disk was created over a long period of time, with deleted files left scattered on various parts of the disk, where they are subsequently filled with newer files. Seeks have to randomly access the files as the disk is backed up in directory order. In this situation, one solution would be to back up all files once, re-create the file system on the device, and then restore all files from tape.

Second, this type of disk access pattern can be seen when multiple processes access different regions of the disk simultaneously, resulting in seeks between the various regions. This can occur if two different file systems on the same disk are backed up simultaneously. In this case, it may be possible to serialize access by scheduling backups in a different manner.

Finally, the outer regions of a disk (lower-numbered cylinders) are faster than the inner regions. Data that needs to be accessed quickly can be written to the outer cylinders.

- *How are disks arranged into logical volumes?*

The logical volume configuration significantly affects performance. To increase levels of performance and reliability to a disk subsystem, you can use some form of logical volume management (either software, or hardware RAID technology).

RAID-0 (striped) volumes can increase overall performance but have the potential to significantly reduce overall volume reliability. Various combinations of RAID-1 (mirroring) and RAID-0 can increase performance while also increasing reliability. RAID-5 can also increase performance and reliability; however, RAID-5 has performance characteristics that you must consider in backup planning. Allocate additional time for data restores to a RAID-5 volume (by a factor of two or three times)—RAID-5 writes take significantly longer than RAID-5 reads, especially with small random writes. (This is true for RAID-5 implemented in software, but not necessarily true for RAID-5 implemented in hardware. For example, the Sun StorEdge A3000 and A3500 storage subsystems provide RAID-5 write rates that are comparable to read rates.) The expected reliability of a logical volume plays a role in determining backup frequency. A RAID volume should be backed up more frequently if any of the following conditions apply:

- The volume has poor reliability (for example, RAID-0 is used).
- The volume is updated frequently.
- The volume contains valuable data.

- *How are disks managed?*

How are individual disks managed or configured into logical volumes? Two ways are with host-based RAID and with hardware RAID.

Host-based RAID systems require more overhead on the server than hardware RAID but are generally more flexible. Volume manager software offers different RAID configuration options (for example, RAID 1+0 versus RAID 0+1). Some volume managers offer additional features, like database snapshots, that can be attractive for backup solutions. A large number of server clients, and most workstation or PC clients, do not use logical volume management but are limited to the performance and reliability characteristics of the individual disk.

- *What are the disk capabilities?*

The capabilities of an individual disk also affect disk subsystem performance and reliability. Newer disks generally run faster and are more reliable than older disks. This is not only because of age but also because of rapid advances in disk technology. During sequential I/O, each disk is capable of specific data transfer rates and random seek rates. When disks are managed as RAID volumes, these capabilities place limitations on overall logical volume performance. Another consideration is the differences in the mean–time–between– failure (MTBF) rates.

Data Destination

When considering the tape subsystem and destination of the data, ask the following questions:

- *What does the tape subsystem look like?*

Although a tape subsystem is a critical component, it is generally less complex than a disk subsystem. Usually, the most difficult tasks associated with a high-performance tape subsystem are the installation and configuration, rather than the planning of the configuration. Planning for tape subsystem capability is often only a matter of using the device specifications to determine storage capacity and throughput characteristics.

- *Where do tape devices reside?*

Determine whether tape devices are to be stand-alone, rack-mounted units that must be loaded by hand or whether they are mounted within a robotic library.

Robotic libraries are the superior choice for enterprise-level backup solutions. Most of the many variations of tape libraries offer multiple tape drive configurations and internal storage capacities in the hundreds of Gbytes.

By knowing the required data capacity, you can plan for sufficient number of libraries to hold the data (include additional capacity for future growth). A reliable solution is to purchase a number of smaller libraries rather than a single large library, since most libraries only have a single robot mechanism.

- *How many tape drives are there?*

Determine how many tape drives will be needed to meet throughput requirements. The tape drives have to be configured, taking into consideration the SCSI or FC-AL slots on the server. If you already have a tape subsystem, determine its capability and, if necessary, supplement it with new equipment. Consider forward and backward compatibility issues with the media, because tape formats change almost as frequently as the underlying hardware.

- *What are the drive capabilities?*

Each type of tape drive has its own characteristics and capabilities. These include native-mode throughput, tape capacity, effectiveness of compression, compatibility of tape formats, and recording inertia. Throughput and capacity are relatively straightforward, but the other factors need careful consideration.

The compression ratio achieved depends on the type of data and the compression algorithm implemented by the drive hardware. For example, the DLT7000 tape drive algorithm trades throughput for compaction, whereas the EXB-8900 Mammoth 8 mm drive is the opposite. Not all tape drives are capable of using older media even if the form-factor is identical. Most drives can read tapes written in older formats but cannot write in the older format.

If backup images are to be archived for a number of years, the upgrade path is important. The drive technology will chiefly determine the recording inertia. For example, linear recording technologies like the DLT7000 drive and the STK RedWood drive generally have a stationary read/write head and quickly moving tape. To perform well, these drives should receive data at a specific minimum rate or faster. Helical-scan technologies like the 4 mm and 8 mm tapes have lower recording inertia and are therefore less sensitive to data input rates; however, they have lower throughput capabilities. It is difficult to balance all these factors, but as long as certain minimum requirements are met, a suboptimal choice usually has little real effect on overall performance.

- *How are the tape devices distributed?*

It is important to optimally locate tape devices throughout the facility. Determine where it would be advantageous to attach backup devices directly to servers that host data. Ask the following questions to gain a clearer understanding of the relationship between tape devices and data to be backed up:

- *Are all tape devices attached to the master server?*

  If all tape devices reside on the master server and the bulk of the data is elsewhere, the network must be able to support transfer rates necessary to move data from remote clients to the centralized backup server. This configuration often simplifies day-to-day management but could require complex networking infrastructure and increased network bandwidth.

- *Are tape libraries attached to an important server?*

  An effective approach is to add tape devices to a server that hosts a large quantity of data, then task it with being the backup slave server managed from the centralized master server. With this architecture, the only information communicated over the network between the master and slave server is the file record information. This information consists of about 200 bytes for each file backed up. Both NetBackup and Solstice Backup support this option.

- *How close are tape drives to the data?*

The proximity of tape drives to servers that host the data highlights network bandwidth issues, since shorter network distances generally have higher-speed network links. If the tape devices and servers hosting the data are located within the same datacenter, it may be advantageous to configure a point-to-point link dedicated to backups. This approach can be an important consideration when deciding where to locate the master server in a widely distributed environment, whereas the network architecture and data locations are generally fixed. Ideally, the master server should be located as close as possible to the bulk of the data and, preferably, close to a centralized location within the network topology.

- *What is the tape environment?*

The operating environment influences the reliability and longevity of the tape subsystem. Ask the following questions:

- *What are the temperature and humidity factors?*

Tapes perform best in moderate temperatures and relatively low humidity. The operating temperature affects tape tension and strength, drive part tolerances, and electronic components within the drive. High humidity can adversely affect the longevity of the magnetic coating on the tape, causing tape surfaces to become gummy. Ideal operating conditions are listed on the media packaging. For example, the operating temperature range for a DLT CompacTape IV tape should be between 10 and 40 degrees centigrade. Tapes should be stored at 16 to 32 degrees centigrade with a humidity between 20 percent and 80 percent. For long-term storage (20 years or more), the requirements are more stringent.

- *How often are drive heads cleaned?*

Drive heads need to be cleaned periodically because they become contaminated with tape deposit. Use head-cleaning tapes for that purpose. Tape drives operated in an unclean environment will require head cleaning more frequently or may suffer failure. New tapes often contain manufacturing debris on their surface, so tape drives that regularly use new tapes should be cleaned frequently. Backup software and tape library hardware can automatically insert cleaning tapes after a drive has been used a number of times.

- *How old are drives and tapes?*

As drives and tapes are used, they eventually wear and produce errors more frequently. Each tape technology has an associated MTBF rate. Each form of tape media can sustain a number of passes before it is expected to wear out. Note that statistics provided by manufacturers are generally optimistic.

The Data Path

When considering the path that data takes as it is copied from disk to tape, ask the following questions:

- *Are data and tapes local to backup servers?*

If data and tapes are local to backup servers, the focus of configuration and tuning should be on moving data quickly between devices and on supporting the potentially large number of processes involved in managing backup streams. These considerations generally fall into two areas: effective memory usage and support for a sufficient amount of local host, or remote procedure call (RPC), capacity.

- *Is the file system buffer cache used?*

Backups are more efficient when the file system buffer cache is bypassed. You can bypass the buffer cache by using Direct I/O to access file systems or by backing up raw volumes instead of file systems. It is better to bypass the system buffer cache for backup streams because the data will not be reused and the cache tends to fill rapidly.

- *How much system memory is available?*

System memory is used when the file system data is buffered into the buffer cache. The buffer cache competes with processes for memory. Adding more memory can temporarily alleviate the problem. However, because the size of backup data is often much larger than the size of system memory, at some point during a long backup process the buffer cache will fill and cause memory contention.

The virtual memory management algorithms in releases prior to the Solaris 8 operating environment did not distinguish between buffer cache memory pages and other pages. This further aggravated the problem of memory contention because process pages could get swapped out to make room for the buffer cache pages. The enhanced virtual memory management algorithm of the Solaris 8 operating environment significantly improves this situation—buffer cache pages will not displace other pages.

Another solution is to avoid the buffer cache altogether by using Direct I/O.

- *What backup software is used?*

  The efficiency of the backup software determines how fast data is moved from disk to tape. Both NetBackup and Solstice Backup move data very efficiently. The Solaris software utilities such as `tar` and `ufsdump` are not as efficient and should not be used to implement enterprise backup solutions.

- Are *data and backup servers distributed across the network?*

  If the data is dumped to tape by a network, ask the following questions:

  - *What kind of network is it?*

    Although networks are generally described in terms of bandwidth, not all networks behave in the same manner. Different networking technologies have different properties. Ethernet variants are inexpensive and common, but their range is generally limited to local area networks. Within a local area network, different topologies offer different performance characteristics. For example, switched Ethernet handles heavy traffic better than a shared segment Ethernet.

  - *What is the available network bandwidth?*

    A typical enterprise network consists of multiple segments and uses a variety of different network technologies. Network bandwidth can vary greatly from one client to another. The available bandwidth for each pathway between the backup server and client needs to be estimated—this can be accomplished by constructing a detailed map of the network.

  - *How many clients share the network simultaneously?*

    If many clients are backed up at the same time, the network is likely to become congested. Conversely, if many clients are backed up simultaneously, the level of multiplexing can be increased. Simultaneous backup enables multiple clients to stream to a single tape, which is advantageous where a single client may be too slow to feed data to the tape at the sufficient rate.

Enterprise Backup Requirements

Backup requirements generally revolve around a few basic issues, primarily the following:

- Backing up data within a time constraint
- Restoring data as needed
- Limiting impact of the backup process on day-to-day operations

Thoroughly research these requirements before recommending a solution. Ask the following questions:

- *What is the backup time window?*

  Determine when backups need to be performed and how long they should take. However, there may not be an ideal time period. Some applications and services must be available 24 hours a day, 7 days a week. In these cases, you must use other methods of obtaining a consistent backup. In other situations, the time required to perform a backup may exceed the time of server inactivity, so consider the following compromises:

  - Decrease frequency of backups.
  - Accept a lower level of data availability.
  - Accept a decrease in application performance.

- *When is access to data least likely?*

  The best time to create a backup opportunity is when demand for data is light, commonly, at night or on weekends. However, there may be other periods of time when system activity is low (for example, lunch times, after quarterly processing is completed, and during holidays). If these periods of inactivity are insufficient, consider how or when these periods can be extended.

- *How much data is to be backed up (full and incremental?)*

  For consistency and recovery purposes, an ideal backup saves the full dataset. The downside to this approach is that full datasets can be very large, consuming time and tape capacity. It is common to perform full backups at weekly or monthly intervals and supplement those with frequent incremental backups that save only data that has changed.

  NetBackup offers a number of incremental backup options. Differential backups record files that have changed since the last backup (either full or incremental). Cumulative backups record all files that have changed since the last full backup. A drawback of cumulative backups is that they record more data than a differential backup. However, an advantage is that a restore operation need only retrieve the last full backup and the last cumulative backup, rather than fetching the last full backup and, potentially, several incremental backups.

Solstice Backup offers similar features, including multiple levels of cumulative backups similar to the levels used by ufsdump(1M). By knowing potential backup targets and the data usage pattern at the site, you can estimate how much data is to be saved during each type of backup. Estimate the data transfer rate by dividing the amount of data by the length of time available for the backup. For added control, you can build various margins for error into the calculations.

- *What is the acceptable impact of performing backups?*

If the window of inactivity is insufficient to save the required volume of data (given available resources and budgetary constraints), then analyze the impact of performing backups concurrently with normal system use. A number of options are available to minimize the impact. Evaluate all options, and select the most appropriate for a given environment.

- *Is data unavailability acceptable?*

The main consideration is the time period when data would be unavailable to users. If the time period is acceptable to users, determine how best to use the time to perform the backup. When data is offline, it can usually be backed up more quickly than when data remains online. Common ways to take data offline include shutting down a database and backing up the underlying raw partitions, or unmounting a file system and backing up the underlying devices.

- *Is degraded performance acceptable?*

If data must be continually available but degradation of overall system performance is acceptable, one choice is to allow backups to continue during normal user activity. A number of mechanisms perform online backups, and each has a different impact on system performance. The method chosen may involve tradeoffs that you need to assess.

- *How long is degraded performance acceptable?*

If data unavailability or degraded performance is acceptable for some period of time, determine what that time period is. Usually the acceptable period of time for data unavailability is less than for degraded performance. Because lower performance may lead to lower productivity, it should be minimized.

- *Are appropriate database modules available?*

Not all commercial databases provide backup modules for NetBackup and Solstice Backup. If hot database backups (or hot backups of commercial applications) need to be performed, ensure the appropriate module is available.

- *What availability concerns should a solution address?*

Any solution should address real concerns and objectives within the enterprise. It is important to understand availability issues that the backup architecture should address. For example, a good solution for recovering files accidentally deleted may be in place; however, it may not be the best solution for recovering an entire site. When analyzing these issues, ask the following questions:

- *Is it critical to minimize impact of user or operator error?*

  If the major concern is the loss of individual files, design a solution to retrieve files quickly with minimal effort for administration. Minor issues can include tape storage, duplicate media, and offsite import/export. An important issue is backup frequency—the copy on tape should be as close as possible to the final state of a file. The level of multiplexing can be high, since overall throughput is not an issue when restoring a small set of files, unless the files are very large.

  To address such issues, you might choose a disk-based, rather than tape-based, solution. Such solutions can include keeping a third mirror of the volume offline and readable in case a file must be restored, or backing up important files to a disk directory rather than to tape.

- *Is it critical to minimize impact from loss of equipment?*

  If the goal is to minimize the impact of failed hardware (for example, a disk head crash), you can structure backups so that data is not kept on the same equipment or on the same set of media. Tape media can be duplicated for additional protection.

  The impact of hardware failure is also relevant in clustered configurations or other systems designed for high availability. Configuring backup architecture for these environments is potentially difficult and requires careful planning. In situations where an entire system needs to be highly available, a solution may be to involve a specialty contractor such as Comdisco.

- *Is it critical to minimize the impact of disasters?*

  Disaster recovery preparation must encompass all aspects of the operation, including training of datacenter personnel. It is common practice to keep multiple copies of media, one local and another archived at a remote site. Another solution is to set up a separate "hot site" where data is imported by the backup software. This site can be ready to restore data within minutes of a disaster. The hot site configuration should have the same capabilities as the primary site. For additional information on disaster recovery, see the Sun BluePrint book *Business Continuity Planning*.

Expectations

It is important to develop realistic expectations when planning a backup architecture. This section discusses potential areas of confusion in the planning that could result in a disproportionate number of problems.

Compression

Data compression has two effects. It speeds up the effective data transfer rate, and it compacts data written to tape, enabling the tape to hold more information.

Compression can be problematic for a number of reasons. The benefits of compression vary, depending on the type of data to be compressed and the compression mechanism used. When the same compression algorithm is used, different types of data compress to different degrees. The level of compression depends on how much redundancy can be identified and remapped in the time available. Some data types, for example, MPEG video, have little or no redundancy to eliminate and, therefore, do not compress well regardless of which compression mechanism is used. By contrast, raw video compresses reasonably well in most cases.

Hardware compression typically used in a tape drive relies on a buffer where data is held temporarily while being compressed. The size of the buffer places limitations on how much data can be examined for redundant patterns. Also, the amount of time necessary to locate all redundant patterns may not be available to the compression mechanism since compression happens in real time, when data is streamed onto the tape.

Administrators often expect either the 2:1 compression ratio frequently quoted in the tape literature, or compression ratios similar to utilities such as compress(1) or GNUzip. This 2:1 compression value has been touted by manufacturers as "typical," when in reality, the value is only typical with the test pattern algorithms used by the manufacturer. The compression ratios of diverse types of data can often be lower. Performance planning based around the 2:1 compression ratio may well be inadequate for the task.

Another common mistake is to use software to compress data and then use that compression ratio to estimate the hardware compression ratio. Software compression and hardware compression are inherently different. Software compression utilities can use all the system memory to perform compression and are under no time constraints. Conversely, hardware compression is constrained by the hardware buffer size and is also limited because compression must be performed in real time. The compression ratio delivered by software utilities is generally better than drive hardware compression.

Compression ratios for various types of data (as observed in simple tests) are shown in TABLE 4-1. For hardware compression, a realistic compression ratio would be closer to 1.4:1, although some data types appear to do better. When data with little or no redundancy (MPEG, JPEG) is backed up, hardware compression should be turned off.

TABLE 4-1   Typical Compression Ratios

Mode	Speedup Ratio	Compaction Ratio
None	1:1	1:1
Text	1.46:1	1.44:1
Motion JPG	0.93:1	0.92:1
Database	1.60:1	1.57:1
File Server	1.60:1	1.63:1
Web Server	1.57:1	1.82:1
Aggregate	1.32:1	1.39:1

Metadata Overhead

Any backup plan must allow for the metadata overhead (above the data itself). Backup software keeps a catalog of files that reside on tape, with a record for each instance of a file. An estimated 150 to 200 bytes are needed per file record. Solstice Backup software typically requires slightly more byte allocation than does NetBackup. A catalog containing a million file records typically requires between 143 and 191 Mbytes of additional space for metadata. Plan to allocate fast and reliable disk space to accommodate the catalog, and include a schedule to back up the catalog itself.

Backup software also writes a certain amount of metadata to tape in order to track what is being written and its location. However, the amount of metadata is usually small in comparison to the dataset size. Tests indicate that metadata written to tape by NetBackup and Solstice Backup is commonly below 1 percent. Other software (for example, ufsdump) may write more metadata to tape, depending on the format used.

Recovery Performance

A common misconception assumes restore performance is identical to backup performance. It was a rule of thumb to anticipate a restore taking three times longer than the corresponding backup. Although this was a safe metric to use, recent measurements indicate that it is too conservative for the latest software and systems from Sun. With correct tuning and adequate hardware support, it is possible to implement restore procedures only 10 percent slower than backup procedures. However, without additional information being available, it may be safer to use a value between 50 percent and 75 percent.

The performance discrepancy between backups and restores exists largely because disk writes often take longer than disk reads. Also, there is more demand for disk writes to be performed synchronously (to guarantee consistency). For example, creating files requires several synchronous writes to update the metadata that tracks file information.

Restore time is increased because of a browse delay occurring at the start of a request. When a restore request is initialized, the software will browse the file record database and locate all records that need to be retrieved. This takes time, especially in a large database containing millions of records.

The situation is more complicated in multiplexed restores because the software usually waits until all restore requests are received before initiating the restore. Alternatively, the software may retrieve files requested after the restore begins. A time delay occurs as file retrieval is synchronized. This synchronization is necessary as data could be distributed across the media. If file retrieval was not synchronized, the restore operation must be serialized—resulting in repeated rewinding of the tape to access individual backup streams.

Ease of Use and Training Requirements

Storage management software has powerful features which can be accessed through the GUI. Library hardware has also been streamlined for ease of use (for example, the GUI touch-screen controls on the Sun StorEdge L3500 tape library). However, "ease of use" does not necessarily equate to "easy to use." Backup and data protection implementation can be highly complex. Decisions made at the planning, installation, and operator levels affect the success of the overall system. Therefore, all involved in the process must either possess the skills required or receive training for the appropriate hardware, software, or issues involved.

It would be naive to expect a well-tuned backup solution could be put together by just assembling the hardware and installing the software. Even a moderately complex backup installation requires experienced personnel to install, configure, and tune various components. This process can take anywhere from days to a few weeks, depending on the complexity of the installation.

One approach is to contract with experienced consultants. For example, Sun, Legato, and others offer professional contract staff who will install and configure a system to specific requirements. This service can include on-site training of personnel to operate and maintain the system. In addition to this basic training, the staff should have further training that enables them to modify the system configuration to deal with changing demands. Alternatively, instead of training staff, you could use a long-term contract that includes system tuning to meet the changing demands of a system.

Simple Sizing Model

This section describes a simple sizing model that can be used to analyze and plan a backup and restore architecture. Many variables in a backup and restore architecture can affect the performance of the system, for example, the size of the current dataset, instantaneous network bandwidth, and resource contention. Modelling these can be difficult and is likely to prove inaccurate since many assumptions would have to be made about changing conditions. Backup and restore architecture can also be tested empirically. However, empirical tests can be time consuming and costly when you are setting up hardware and software. What is needed is a simple sizing model that can show the theoretical, nominal, and pragmatic limits of the architecture. Architectural changes and what-if scenarios can be tested against the model to see any effects they may have before you invest in the products.

Before detailing the model, we discuss the following topics:

- General backup and restore workload characteristics
- Performance characteristics of the four major hardware components used to build the model (network, I/O channel, disk, tape)

Workload Characteristics

Backup and restore workloads have characteristics that allow reduction of the problem set:

- Large, bulk transfers of data
- Sequential ordering of data
- Few opportunities for short-term data reuse

These characteristics allow the model to be simplified (as the caches will be discounted from the equation). Much of the design of a modern computer system centers around optimizing cache use. For example, a modern microprocessor may have 3 to 10 caches in its architecture, RAID arrays may have several caches, operating systems have caches, and disk and tape drives have caches. Most of these cache designs are optimized for *temporal locality*—most recently accessed items that are likely to be accessed again in the near future. The very nature of backups or restores is counter to temporal locality—the data will be copied to the backup media and not needed again for some time.

Caches also tend to be relatively small. The size of a cache is almost always dictated by the cost of building the cache, which usually has a high cost per bit. Conversely, tape archives are generally inexpensive, with a low cost per bit. It is economical to put most of the data on the lower-priced medium than on the higher-priced medium. The end result is that there tends to be much more data in total than will fit in the caches.

Therefore, caches are not effective for most backup and restore workloads because they inefficiently store data that will not be reused and they are far too small to store the entire dataset. Eliminating caches for data storage simplifies the model because without caches, the lowest bandwidth bottleneck in the system will be exposed. It is this bottleneck that must be identified.

Network Sizing

Accurately assessing a network can be difficult, due in part to the nature of networks and the rapid expansion of network technology. Each advancement in the technology can have its own characteristics and complex interrelationships. As a network expands, there may be multiple paths between any given points on the network, with each different path offering a different bandwidth. Also, traffic loads tend to be increasing but unpredictable. For example, migrating a legacy terminal-based service to a new internet-based service may dramatically alter the traffic loads across an enterprise network. These are some of the challenging factors that planners can face.

Sometimes it can be easier to plan dedicated backup and restore architecture from scratch rather than to modify an existing architecture. However, adding such networks may involve installing additional wiring between distant parts of the enterprise, which is more expensive than the cost of switches and adapters. Either way, planners must understand how to use the existing infrastructure to meet any new demands placed on the backup system.

A well-designed storage architecture may dedicate a network to the backup function. This is generally a good idea since the large data transfer workload used for backup and restore can easily consume the bandwidth of the network. This has a negative performance impact on short, bursty, and response-time-sensitive workloads typically found in networks supporting user interaction.

There are some basic techniques that can be used to effectively perform network capacity planning for backup and restore workloads. The goal is to configure sufficient bandwidth between the data location and tape device. TABLE 4-2 lists the performance rates of some technologies used for a backup and restore workload.

TABLE 4-2   Estimated Performance Rates for Network Technologies

Technology	Theoretical Speed Mbit/sec	Nominal Speed Mbyte/sec
Modem	0.056	0.004
ISDN	0.128	0.010
Frame Relay 256	0.256	0.020
Frame Relay 512	0.512	0.039
T-1	1.54	0.115
T-3	44.7	3.4
Ethernet (10baseT)	10.0	1.0
FastEthernet (100baseT)	100.0	8.0
GigabitEthernet (1000baseT)	1000.0	50.0
FDDI	100.0	8.0
CDDI	100.0	8.0
ATM 155	155.0	11.0
ATM 622	622.0	50.0
HIPPI-s	800.0	60.0
Interdomain Networking	—	60.0

Note – Units used to describe network and storage bandwidth are generally different. Network bandwidth is usually listed as *Mb/second* or *Mbps*, and refers to 1000 x 1000 *bits* per second. In contrast, storage bandwidth is usually listed as *MB/second* or *MB/s*, and refers to 1024 x 1024 *bytes* per second. For example, a storage bandwidth of 1 Mbyte/sec is equivalent to network bandwidth of 8.39 Mbits/sec.

Many businesses have a significant investment in their existing network infrastructure. With the high cost of installing additional wiring, it may be preferable to strategically place backup servers in locations where the existing networks can be used.

The first step is to produce a map of the existing network showing all network links and their relationship to one another. Individual links can be labeled with their anticipated bandwidth requirement during the projected backup window. The full bandwidth required by the link may not be available for the backup because networks are usually shared with other users. Network administrators commonly keep usage statistics that identify any quiet times in the network; include this information in the map. Determine how much backup data will be generated at server and segment levels. Servers that host a large amount of data are candidate "hotspots" that you may need to relocate or tune to better suit conditions.

Once you have constructed a map of existing network infrastructure, determine the lowest bandwidth link between each backup client and server. This information will be used in the model.

Next, locate the central point in the network. This point has the maximum amount of bandwidth available and the minimum number of hops to the data. This central point is an ideal location to place the master server.

Channel Sizing

Channel sizing is used in the model to expose bottlenecks that may be hidden in the I/O interconnects—between the host and disks, RAID arrays, tapes, and interconnects internal to RAID arrays. For most RAID arrays, the interconnect to the host is the typical bottleneck. For example, an A3500 RAID array contains five UltraSCSI channels for its disks but only two UltraSCSI channels for connection to the host. The bottleneck is assumed to be the connection to the host for this simple model. TABLE 4-3 contains bandwidth information for a number of channel technologies.

TABLE 4-3   Channel Sizing Bandwidth

Channel Technology	Peak Theoretical Throughput (Mbyte/sec)		Nominal Throughput (Mbyte/sec)	
	Read	Write	Read	Write
Narrow, Sync SCSI	10	10	8	8
Fast, wide SCSI	20	20	17	17
UltraSCSI	40	40	35	35
Fiber Channel (FC-25)	25	25	18	16
Fiber Channel (FC-AL)	100	100	95	95
SPARCStorage Array (SSA)	25	25	18	16

TABLE 4-3 Channel Sizing Bandwidth

Channel Technology	Peak Theoretical Throughput (Mbyte/sec)		Nominal Throughput (Mbyte/sec)	
A1000	40	40	28	20
A3500	80	80	60	41
A5000	100	100	95	76

Disk Drive Sizing

Disks are usually the source of data for backup operations, (disk reads) and the destination of data for restore operations (disk writes). Disks generally read faster than they write. Both read and write performance is important to the model since both backup *and* restore operations need to be analyzed.

Disks should be configured and tuned for their primary purpose and then adjusted for backup and restore. When planning a new system from scratch, it makes sense to plan the primary and backup activities jointly.

For backup and restore operations, the key metric is disk bandwidth because the transfers tend to be large and sequential. Disk performance will typically be close to the rate at which the data can be passed between the heads and the medium. As disk technology improves (storage density and rotational speed), this bottleneck may move to the channel used to connect to the disk (unless the channels are also improved).

Disk RAID arrays are not considered as disk sizing in this simple model. The RAID arrays are really just collections of disks with additional channels and caches. The channels are covered separately and the caches are already removed from consideration.

TABLE 4-4 shows read and write performance for disks commonly found in systems today. This list is not exhaustive, because new, faster disks, which will outdate the table, are released continuously. However, these numbers do represent a reasonable estimate for disk technologies if the actual data is not readily available.

TABLE 4-4   Estimated Performance Rates for Disk Technology

Disk Size (Gbytes)	Rotational Speed (rpm)	Peak Read Throughput (Mbyte/sec)	Peak Write Throughput (Mbyte/sec)
4	5,400	5.6	2.8
4	7,200	9.3	4.2
9	7,200	8.7	4.1
9	10,000	11 – 16	Not Specified
18	7,200	14 – 21	Not Specified

Tape Drive Sizing

Tape drive sizing is similar to disk drive sizing in that the key bottleneck is generally the rate at which data can be passed between the heads and medium. Tape drives add complexity to the calculations because of three indeterminate characteristics: compression, back-hitching, and tape changing. Compression can improve performance because it can reduce the amount of data actually written to the medium. Back-hitching can significantly decrease performance as a result of insufficient amounts of data being transferred between the host and tape drive. Changing tapes can take a significant amount of time if done manually. Robotic changers can change tapes in a predictable time frame, but are susceptible to contention because typically only one robot serves a number of tape drives. It is difficult to model these effects, so they are not directly addressed by this simple model.

Advertised native rates can be used to calculate bandwidth available to tape devices. TABLE 4-5 lists capacities and rates for common tape devices. Most devices include some level of hardware compression, which should be taken into account. As a guideline, use a 1.4:1 compression ratio because the 2:1 advertised ratio is usually too optimistic.

TABLE 4-5   Estimated Performance Rates and Capacities for Tape Drives

Device	Capacity (Mbytes)		Throughput (Mbyte/sec)	
	1:1 (Uncompressed)	1.4:1 (Compressed)	1.1 (Uncompressed)	1.4:1 (Compressed)
DDS-3	12	16.8	1	1.4
Exabyte 8900	20	28	3	4.2
DLT 7000	35	49	5	7
STK 9840	20	28	9	12.6
STK RedWood	50	71.5	10.5	14.7
IBM 3490	0.2	N/A	3	N/A
IBM 3590E	0.4	0.56	6	8.4

Tape libraries contain one or more tape drives and an automated robot to change tapes. TABLE 4-6 lists a variety of tape libraries and their capabilities. Tape library performance is not explicitly used in this simple sizing model; rather, the drives used in the libraries are used.

TABLE 4-6   Estimated Performance Rates and Capacities for Tape Libraries

Library	Drive Type	No. Drives	Slots	Capacity (Mbytes)		Throughput (Gbyte/hr)	
				1:1	1.4:1	1:1	1.4:1
DDS-3 Autoloader	DDS-3	1	6	72	100	3.5	4.9
L280	DLT	1	8	280	392	17.6	24.6
L400	Exabyte	2	20	400	560	21.1	29.5
L1000	DLT	4	30	1,000	1,400	70.3	98.4
L3500	DLT	7	100	3,500	4,900	123.0	172.3
L11000	DLT	16	326	11,000	15,400	281.3	393.8
L700	DLT	20	690	24,150	19,320	360.0	504.0
L700	9840	12	690	13,800	33,810	388.8	544.3

The Simple Sizing Model at Work

The simple sizing model looks for a bottleneck in the backup and restore architecture. This bottleneck provides an expected backup and restore throughput value, which can then be used to determine the total amount of time required to complete a backup and restore operation. This model can also be used to explore alternate remedies for the bottleneck. Although there will always be some bottleneck in the system, it is worthwhile to explore the effects of changing parts of the system architecture.

The model looks at both backup and restore performance simultaneously, so you can see the impact of design decisions and separate the truth from the marketing hype of system component suppliers.

The model builds a path from data media (usually disk) to backup media (usually tape). This path comprises up to four basic components: network, channels, disks, and tapes. FIGURE 4-1 shows the typical structure for locally attached tape drive design; FIGURE 4-2 shows the structure for a network-attached drive.

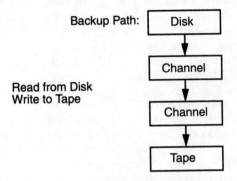

FIGURE 4-1   Typical Structure for Locally Attached Tape Drive.

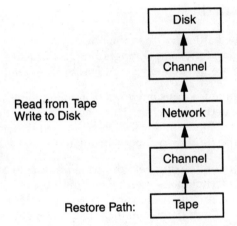

FIGURE 4-2   Typical Structure for Network-Attached Tape Drive

To keep the model simple, we use only the lowest bandwidth component or link in the design. For example, if there are three network hops between the tape and the disk—Ethernet, T1, and FastEthernet—then the slower T1 would be used for the model.

The design is complete when the lowest bandwidth component meets the design requirements. If it does not meet your design requirements, then you must evaluate other remedies. This becomes an iterative process: remedies are applied and the model evaluated until the design requirements are met.

Multiplexing as a Remedy

Multiplexing is a common remedy for bandwidth problems. Multiplexing allows multiple data streams to occur in parallel. This behavior is useful when multiple, low bandwidth data streams are multiplexed onto a higher bandwidth data stream. Multiplexing is why RAID disk systems using RAID-0 or RAID-5 can attain higher throughput than simple disks. For disks, the bottleneck is commonly the throughput of moving data from the channel to the media. This throughput is almost always less than the channel throughput. Placing multiple disk drives on a single channel increases the channel bandwidth use.

Multiplexing can take several forms. For disks, both RAID and multiple concurrent backup streams can achieve the same goal: increasing the total throughput to the tape system. Networks can be trunked to form parallel paths. Channels can be added and used with RAID or multiple streams. Finally, multiple tape drives can be driven with multiple streams. It is common to use multiplexing at several component levels to achieve high-speed backup and restore requirements.

Network Remedies

If a network is the bottleneck, then the obvious remedy is to use an alternate network technology, for example, upgrading from 10baseT to 100baseT Ethernet. However, sometimes this remedy is not feasible, especially for a WAN network.

Multiplexing techniques can sometimes be applied to networks. Sun supports trunking of some network devices. Trunking aggregates the bandwidth across two or more interfaces. However, any switches or network equipment connected to the interfaces must also be able to support trunking.

Another method of optimizing network bandwidth is to back up multiple clients concurrently. This technique is useful when multiple clients are connected by a WAN. For example, multiple clients connected by ISDN to a single backup server can support many clients before another component becomes the bottleneck.

Compression can be used at the network layer. In this model, client-side compression is described in the network layer as an increase in the network bandwidth because data stored on disk is not usually compressed. Tape drives have a compression function built into the hardware. Client-side compression fits well in the network layer for this model since that is where the most benefit can be gained.

Adding a slave tape server to a network is a good idea if the network bottleneck is not in the client's local network, for example, a building with 100baseT Ethernet for local traffic and a 10baseFX Ethernet connection to the datacenter that contains the backup server. In such a case, adding a slave tape server to the building's network can improve performance. Solstice Backup and Veritas NetBackup can easily administer such slave servers from a central location.

Channel Remedies

Channel remedies can be the most difficult to apply directly. The reason is that the cost of migrating from low bandwidth channels to high bandwidth channels can be expensive or impractical, especially when disk or tape components do not support the higher bandwidth channel. Adding additional channels to any of the other components can also increase costs significantly. The most practical remedy is to use additional channels. For example, if the model has determined that the channel connecting the disk drive is the bottleneck but the disk drive does not support a faster channel, the remedy could be to add a second channel and second disk drive. The data is then multiplexed across the two disk drives.

Disk Remedies

There are few remedies for bottlenecks at disk level. Compression is not typically used in the UNIX industry at disk level. At one time, file compression was used in the personal computer industry; however, it has fallen by the wayside as the cost of disks continues to fall. Multiplexing can take the form of RAID-0 or RAID-5 volumes. Multiplexing also supports the case of using multiple streams to back up multiple disks concurrently.

Upgrading disks to faster models is also possible. However, the rate of increase in data transfer speed in the disk drive industry tends to lag behind the rest of the computer component industries. Doubling the performance of disk drives occurs perhaps once every four to five years. Using multiplexing techniques can double the performance of a volume immediately and is the preferred choice of many system planners.

Tape Remedies

The description of increased performance over time for tape drives is similar to that of disk drives. Tape drives can perform data compression before writing the data to tape. For compressible data, this effectively results in more bits per inch recorded to the tape media. Almost all modern tape drives support compression.

Tape drives can also be multiplexed. The complexities involved in tape management for data spread across multiple tapes tends to discourage multiplexing a single stream onto multiple tape drives concurrently. However, high-performance tape drives that can often store and retrieve data faster than other components in the system are readily available.

Examples

This section contains examples of a simple tape sizing model used to examine backup and restore architecture. The first case describes a locally attached disk and tape. (See FIGURE 4-3 and TABLE 4-7) The second case examines backup and restore across a LAN. The third case considers backup and restore across a WAN.

Example 1: Locally Attached Tape and Disk Drives

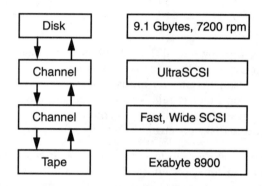

Backup = ↓   Restore = ↑

FIGURE 4-3   Simple Sizing Model — Locally Attached Disk and Tape

TABLE 4-7   Sizing Information for Locally Attached Disk and Tape

Component	Peak Throughput (Mbyte/sec)		Nominal Throughput (Mbyte/sec)	
	Read	Write	Read	Write
9.1-Gbyte, 7200 rpm Disk	8.7	4.1	8.7	4.1
UltraSCSI	40.0	40.0	35.0	35.0
Fast, Wide SCSI	20.0	20.0	17.0	17.0
Exabyte 8900 tape (Uncompressed)	3.0	3.0	3.0	3.0
Exabyte 8900 tape (Compressed, 1.4:1)	4.2	4.2	4.2	4.2

The bottleneck is immediately obvious: the Exabyte 8900 tape drive. However, the tape drive bottleneck affects the backup time more than the restore time. If compression is used on the tape drive, then the bottleneck for restoring the data may occur at the disk drive. Unfortunately, it is nearly impossible to predict the actual compression ratio since it is data dependent. This simple sizing model provides a good view into bottlenecks in the system. A more detailed model would probably be less useful than actually running a backup and restore test and measuring the throughput and completion times.

The total size of the data to be backed up is needed to complete the analysis. The worst case would be a complete raw dump of the entire contents of the disk. The capacity of the 9.1 Gbyte disk drive is approximately 9.1 million 1 Kbyte blocks or about 8.9 Gbytes. The 2.4 percent discrepancy is due to marketing trends in the disk drive industry. The backup and restore time estimations for uncompressed data are listed below:

Backup Time   = Data size / Bottleneck bandwidth (Exabyte 8900)

                          = 8.9 Gbytes / 3 Mbyte/sec

                          = 8900 Mbytes / 3 Mbyte/sec

                          = 2967 seconds

                          = 49 minutes 27 seconds

Restore Time   = Data size / Bottleneck bandwidth (Exabyte 8900)

                          = 8.9 Gbytes / 3 Mbyte/sec

                          = 49 minutes 27 seconds

If compression is used and assuming a 1.4:1 compression ratio, the estimates change as follows:

Backup Time   = Data size / Bottleneck bandwidth (Exabyte 8900)

                          = 8.9 Gbytes / 4.2 Mbyte/sec

                          = 8900 Mbytes / 4.2 Mbyte/sec

                          = 2119 seconds

                          = 35 minutes 19 seconds

Restore Time   = Data size / Bottleneck bandwidth (disk)

                          = 8.9 Gbytes / 4.1 Mbyte/sec

                          = 8900 Mbytes / 4.1 Mbyte/sec

                          = 2171 seconds

                          = 36 minutes 11 seconds

This example shows that the bottleneck may not be with the same component for every situation. If compression is used in the tape drive, the restore time bottleneck may be at the disk drive. The restore time is often more important than the backup time for rapidly recovering a system and should always be analyzed when backup and restore systems are sized.

Example 2: Backup and Restore Across a LAN

FIGURE 4-4 shows the simple sizing model for a client system with locally attached disk, using the network to access the tape drives on a server.

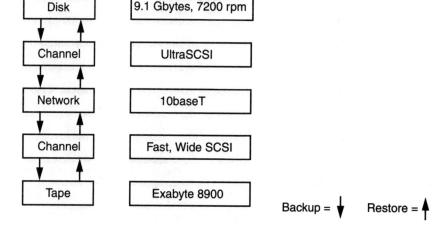

FIGURE 4-4   Backup and Restore Across a LAN

TABLE 4-8 shows the sizing information used for the calculations.

TABLE 4-8   Sizing Information for Backup and Restore Across a LAN

Component	Peak Throughput (Mbyte/sec)		Nominal Throughput (Mbyte/sec)	
	Read	Write	Read	Write
9.1-Gbyte, 7200 rpm Disk	8.7	4.1	8.7	4.1
UltraSCSI	40.0	40.0	35.0	35.0
Fast, Wide SCSI	20.0	20.0	17.0	17.0
10baseT Ethernet	1.1	1.1	1.0	1.0
Exabyte 8900 Tape (Uncompressed)	3.0	3.0	3.0	3.0
Exabyte 8900 Tape (Compressed, 1.4:1)	4.2	4.2	4.2	4.2

In this example, the bottleneck is clearly the 10baseT Ethernet. The backup and restore time nominal performance estimations for uncompressed data are as follows:

Backup Time   = Data size / Bottleneck bandwidth (10baseT Ethernet)

= 8.9 Gbytes / 1 Mbyte/sec

= 8900 Mbytes / 1 Mbyte/sec

= 8900 seconds

= 148 minutes 20 seconds

Restore Time   = Data size / Bottleneck bandwidth (10baseT Ethernet)

= 8.9 Gbytes / 1 Mbyte/sec

= 148 minutes 20 seconds

To improve backup and restore performance, the 10baseT network bottleneck must be resolved. If the network was upgraded to 100baseT, then the bottleneck would shift to the tape or disk drive and the analysis results would be the same as example 1.

Another solution may be to use compression on the client side. Using compression on the client side effectively eliminates the option of using compression on the tape drive. The analysis uses a slightly different table of bandwidth values, as shown in TABLE 4-9.

TABLE 4-9   Sizing Information When Client-Side Compression Is Used

Component	Peak Throughput (Mbyte/sec)		Nominal Throughput (Mbyte/sec)	
	Read	Write	Read	Write
9.1-Gbyte, 10,000 rpm Disk	8.7	4.1	8.7	4.1
UltraSCSI	40.0	40.0	35.0	35.0
Fast, Wide SCSI	20.0	20.0	17.0	17.0
10baseT Ethernet	1.1	1.1	1.0	1.0
10baseT Ethernet (Compressed, 1.4:1)	1.54	1.54	1.4	1.4
Exabyte 8900 Tape (Uncompressed)	3.0	3.0	3.0	3.0

The nominal performance analysis is as follows:

Backup Time   = Data size / Bottleneck bandwidth (10baseT Ethernet)

                  = 8.9 Gbytes / 1.4 Mbyte/sec

                  = 8900 Mbytes / 1.4 Mbyte/sec

                  = 6357 seconds

                  = 105 minutes 57 seconds

Restore Time   = Data size / Bottleneck bandwidth (10baseT Ethernet)

                  = 8.9 Gbytes / 1.4 Mbyte/sec

                  = 105 minutes 57 seconds

This analysis demonstrates that using client-side compression for data when the bottleneck is a slow network can yield a large improvement. In this example, the improvement is more than 40 minutes; however, the improvement does not come without a cost. Client-side compression does consume CPU time. The additional CPU use may negatively impact applications being run on the client during the backup. On the other hand, the restore time is also improved. It is possible that client applications may be down or unavailable while the system is being restored and may be unaffected by the CPU cycles used for the restoration. Improving the restore time by 40 minutes will go far toward improving overall system availability.

This example is also useful for exploring peak performance limits. TABLE 4-9 shows both peak and nominal bandwidth for 10baseT Ethernet. It is useful to analyze peak performance, especially if the bottleneck may move to another component during best-case scenarios.

The peak performance analysis shows the following facts:

Backup Time (Peak) = Data size / Bottleneck bandwidth (10baseT Ethernet)

$\qquad$ = 8.9 Gbytes / 1.1 Mbyte/sec

$\qquad$ = 8900 Mbytes / 1.1 Mbyte/sec

$\qquad$ = 8091 seconds

$\qquad$ = 134 minutes 50 seconds

Restore Time (Peak) = Data size / Bottleneck bandwidth (10baseT Ethernet)

$\qquad$ = 8.9 Gbytes / 1.1 Mbyte/sec

$\qquad$ = 134 minutes 50 seconds

The peak performance analysis for client-side compression is as follows:

Backup Time (Peak) = Data size / Bottleneck bandwidth (10baseT Ethernet)

$\qquad$ = 8.9 Gbytes / 1.54 Mbyte/sec

$\qquad$ = 8900 Mbytes / 1.54 Mbyte/sec

$\qquad$ = 5779 seconds

$\qquad$ = 96 minutes 19 seconds

Restore Time (Peak) = Data size / Bottleneck bandwidth (10baseT Ethernet)

$\qquad$ = 8.9 Gbytes / 1.54 Mbyte/sec

$\qquad$ = 96 minutes 19 seconds

Peak performance analysis is useful in the determination of the upper bounds of the problem. It is clear that the best possible backup and restore times are 96 minutes and 19 seconds. If that does not meet the business requirements, then some component of the architecture must change.

Peak performance analysis is also useful for what-if scenarios. For example, if the tape drive was changed from an Exabyte 8900 to a DDS-3, then the bottleneck may be either the network or the tape drive. TABLE 4-10 shows the results of such an analysis.

TABLE 4-10   Peak Performance Analysis

Case		Backup and Restore (Peak)		Backup and Restore (Nominal)	
Tape Type	Compression	Bottleneck	Time (sec)	Bottleneck	Time (sec)
Exabyte 8900	None	Network	8091	Network	8900
Exabyte 8900	Client-Side	Network	5779	Network	6357
Exabyte 8900	Tape	Network	8091	Network	8900
DDS-3	None	Tape	8900	Network or Tape	8900
DDS-3	Client-Side	Tape	8900	Network	8900
DDS-3	Tape	Network	8091	Network	8900

It is clear from the analysis that replacing Exabyte 8900 with a DDS-3 tape drive would probably not improve the overall performance in this case. However, if the original system had a DDS-3 tape drive and the analysis was performed to determine the effect of replacing it with an Exabyte 8900, then the analysis shows that in some (but not all) cases, replacement would help. This analysis demonstrates the best outcome would be to replace the DDS-3 tape drive with the Exabyte 8900 and to implement client-side compression.

Example 3: Backup and Restore Across a WAN

FIGURE 4-5 shows the simple sizing model for three client systems with locally attached disk using a network to access a single tape drive on a server. This example explores the effect of multiplexing.

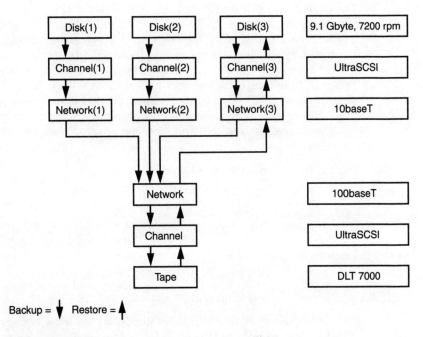

FIGURE 4-5   Simple Sizing Model That Uses Multiplexing

See TABLE 4-11 for sizing information used in calculations.

TABLE 4-11   Sizing Information Used for Calculations

Component	Peak Throughput (Mbyte/sec)		Nominal Throughput (Mbyte/sec)	
	Read	Write	Read	Write
9.1 Gbyte, 7200 rpm Disk	8.7	4.1	8.7	4.1
UltraSCSI	40.0	40.0	35.0	35.0
10baseT Ethernet	1.1	1.1	1.0	1.0
10baseT Ethernet (Compressed)	1.54	1.54	1.4	1.4
100baseT Ethernet	12.0	12.0	8.0	8.0
Exabyte 8900 (Uncompressed)	3.0	3.0	3.0	3.0
Exabyte 8900 (Compressed)	4.2	4.2	4.2	4.2

This system requires more analysis of the different options available. Also, the process must be examined from both the client and server perspective.

The analysis for a case with no compression, three clients, and nominal performance shows that the bottleneck will be either the network or tape. For the backup case, the available bandwidth of the tape drive is 3 Mbyte/sec, whereas the total load generated by the clients is also 3 Mbyte/sec. For the restore case, the bottleneck is the network as the client being restored is limited by the bandwidth of its 10baseT Ethernet. In this case, backup and restore times will be identical: 8900 seconds, as shown in example 2. However, the data rate that is written to tape is 3 Mbyte/sec. The tape drive is doing three times the amount of work of the single client case. Both the client networks and the tape drive are at saturation. The details of this analysis are shown below:

Backup Time   = Data size / Bottleneck bandwidth

                = (3 * 8.9 Gbytes) / (3 * 1 Mbyte/sec)

                = 8900 seconds

                = 148 minutes 20 seconds

Restore Time   = Data size / Bottleneck bandwidth (10baseT Ethernet)

                = 8.9 Gbytes / 1 Mbyte/sec

                = 148 minutes 20 seconds

Note that the restore time is always limited by the slow network on the client side. The only way to improve the situation is to use client-side compression.

To further understand this scenario, let us look at the case where the tape is not saturated. Enabling tape compression can saturate the tape. With a 1.4:1 compression ratio the tape drive will saturate at approximately 4.2 Mbyte/sec. However, the network to each client will saturate at 1 Mbyte/sec. Therefore, with tape compression enabled, the server can accommodate a fourth client without impacting the existing three clients. TABLE 4-12 shows the scenarios available and the bottleneck analysis results.

TABLE 4-12   Multiple Clients Using Single Tape—Analysis

Compression	Backup		Restore		Additional Clients Serviceable
	Bottleneck	Time (sec)	Bottleneck	Time (sec)	
None	Network or Tape	8900	Network	8900	0
Client Side	Tape	8900	Network	6357	0
Tape	Network	8900	Network	8900	1

Consider a case of six clients with no compression: the bottleneck is clearly the tape drive. The analysis is as follows:

Backup Time = Data size / Bottleneck bandwidth (Exabyte 8900)

= (6 * 8.9 Gbytes) / 3 Mbyte/sec

= 17800 seconds

= 296 minutes 40 seconds

Enabling tape compression will improve this case as follows:

Backup Time = Data size / Bottleneck bandwidth (Exabyte 8900)

= (6 * 8.9 Gbytes) / 4.2 Mbyte/sec

= 12714 seconds

= 211 minutes 54 seconds

This analysis demonstrates that improving any bottleneck can improve overall performance. This is especially true where many clients are writing data to a single tape drive.

Other Considerations

Startup Time

Backups of file systems, databases, or other logical data may require some time to gather information to ensure consistency. For file systems, this information may include directory structures and incremental backup timestamp checks. For databases, gathering this information requires collecting the schema information and checking consistency. These operations are not constrained by the backup system bottleneck, but they do impact the wall clock time required to perform the backup.

Other considerations, not described in the simple sizing model, can affect backup and restore performance. The effect of these may vary widely from system to system, and case to case. Some of the considerations commonly encountered are discussed in the following paragraph:

CPU Sizing

To simplify configuration of CPU capacity, estimate the number of CPU cycles required to move data at a certain rate. Experiments have demonstrated a realistic estimate is 5 MHz of UltraSPARC CPU capacity per 1 Mbyte/sec of data to be moved. For example, a system that needs to back up clients over a network to local tape at a rate of 10 Mbyte/sec would need 100 MHz of available CPU power. This calculation includes 50 MHz to move data from the network to the server and another 50 MHz to move data from the server to the tapes. This workload would use approximately 33 percent of a 300 MHz UltraSPARC processor.

As another example, a system needing to back up a database from local disk to a local tape device at a rate of 35 Mbyte/sec would need 350 MHz of CPU power. The software overhead is small and is included in the 5 MHz per Mbyte/sec estimate.

Memory Sizing

General server memory sizing guidelines should be adequate. However, in the case where the total size of system RAM is significantly less than the total size of the files, it may be better to disable the file buffer cache, particularly for releases prior to the Solaris 8 operating environment. The file buffer cache can compete with applications for RAM and causes the operating system to do extra work managing the cached files. The virtual memory paging algorithm was changed in the Solaris 8 operating environment to effectively eliminate the competition between applications and the file buffer cache for RAM. However, it is still a good idea to eliminate unnecessary caching if possible.

UFS Direct I/O

The Solaris 2.6 operating environment added the capability of disabling the file system buffer cache for UFS. Disabling is set with the forcedirectio option to the mount command. It can be set on a per-file system basis at boot time in the /etc/vfstab file or interactively with the mount command. For example:

- Verify current settings.

```
# mount | grep /opt
/opt on /dev/dsk/c0t13d0s0
read/write/setuid/intr/largefiles/logging/onerror=panic/dev=8000
60 on Sat Apr  1 14:22:45 2000
```

The option flags do not contain the forcedirectio keyword.

- Remount, using forcedirectio option, and verify.

```
# mount -o remount,forcedirectio /opt
# mount | grep /opt
/opt on /dev/dsk/c0t13d0s0
read/write/setuid/intr/forcedirectio/largefiles/onerror=panic/de
v=800060 on Sun Apr 16 21:16:13 2000
```

The forcedirectio option is set, disabling the file buffer cache.

- Perform file system backup.

■ Enable file buffer cache and verify.

```
# mount -o remount,noforcedirectio /opt
# mount | grep /opt
/opt on /dev/dsk/c0t13d0s0
read/write/setuid/intr/noforcedirectio/largefiles/onerror=panic/
dev=800060 on Sun Apr 16 21:36:33 2000
```

The forcedirectio option is not set, enabling file system buffer cache.

Tape Back-Hitching

Tape back-hitching occurs when the data is being transferred to or from the tape faster than it is being transferred to or from the tape drive. Back-hitching is prevalent in the writing to tape case because the operating system can buffer data being read from the tape. The tape must stop, rewind, and start again. This mechanical action can take several seconds, depending on the tape drive. Several seconds can be several Mbytes of data. To eliminate tape back-hitching, ensure that the tape drive is not the bottleneck in the system.

Tape Changing

Tape changing can also negatively impact performance. The tape may have to rewind, go offline, schedule the robot, be ejected, move to its slot; then, another tape must be loaded. The time required to perform these operations may be on the order of minutes, depending on the robotic mechanism, slot location, and robotics contention. Unfortunately, it is difficult to predict the time required for such changes. It is best to accommodate the tape changes required for a large data backup task based on experience or measured results.

Media Errors

Media errors for tape drives are handled by rewriting the data. This eliminates the need for preformatted tapes at the cost of indeterminate capacity and write throughput. Most tape drives will not report errors to the operating system unless many errors are detected on the media. Thus, the system administrator may not be aware of a media problem unless it is a major problem. However, the performance will be impacted since the data will have to be written more than once to the media. The best solution is to use high-quality media, follow tape drive maintenance procedures, and ensure proper environmental conditions for the media and tape drives.

## CHAPTER 5

NetBackup Runbook

This chapter provides step-by-step procedures, in runbook format. These procedures can be helpful in environments using VERITAS NetBackup. Sun offers an OEM version of NetBackup called Sun StorEdge Enterprise NetBackUp.

Note – In this chapter, the term NetBackup refers to VERITAS NetBackup, although the information provided here also applies to Sun StorEdge Enterprise NetBackUp.

Runbooks are useful for standardizing day-to-day operations throughout an IT organization.

Additional runbooks related to backup and restore practices (and many other topics) are available from Sun Professional Services. These include VERITAS NetBackup runbooks, Solstice Backup runbooks, and other backup and restore runbooks. Sun Professional Services can customize runbooks for your particular environment. For additional information on runbooks, see:

`http://www.sun.com/service/sunps`.

This chapter presents only a portion of a NetBackup Runbook available. Additional topics available in this runbook include:

1. Storage Units
   - To Add a Media Manager Storage Unit
   - To Add a UNIX Disk-Filesystem Storage Unit
   - To Change Storage Unit Attributes
   - To Delete a Storage Unit
   - To Display Storage Unit Attributes

2. Media Manager
   - To Run the Media Manager GUI
   - Reference: Media Manager Main Window Menu

- Reference: Media Manager Configuration File

3. Volumes
   - To Add a New Volume Pool
   - To Change Volume Pool Attributes
   - To Delete a Volume Pool
   - To Change a Volume Pool Assignment for a Volume
   - To Reassign Media to a Different Pool
   - To Configure a Scratch Pool
   - To Add Robotic Volumes (with Update Volume Configuration)
   - To Add a Single Volume (without Update Volume Configuration)
   - To Move a Volume Group
   - To Delete Single or Multiple Volumes
   - To Delete a Volume Group
   - To De-assign Regular Backup Volumes
   - To De-assign Database Backup Volumes
   - To Change Volume Attributes

4. Replacing Media
   - To Replace Media without Reusing the Media ID
   - To Replace Media and Reuse the Media ID
   - To Reuse Media with the Same Media ID
   - To Reuse Media with a New Media ID

5. Tape Drive Operations
   - To Run the Device Manager GUI
   - To Change the Operation Mode of a Drive
   - To Unload a Drive
   - To Terminate a Drive Assignment
   - To Reset a Drive
   - To Add Comments for a Drive
   - To Configure Drive Cleaning
   - To Change Drive Cleaning Frequency
   - To Manually Start a Drive Cleaning Operation
   - To Reset Mount Time to Zero

6. NetBackup Classes
   - Reference: Class Attributes
   - To Create a New Class
   - To Add Clients to a Class
   - To Add or Delete Clients from Multiple Classes
   - To Add a New Schedule to a Class
   - Reference: Schedule Attributes
   - To Define the List of Files to Backup
   - Reference: File Path Rules for Standard UNIX wbak Clients
   - Reference: Symbolic Links and Hard Links

Monitoring and Killing Backup Jobs

▼ To Obtain Status

1. **Log in to the master Netbackup server as the system administrator.**

2. **Run this command:**

```
# /usr/openv/netbackup/bin/xnb -d display &
```

A GUI with the following buttons is displayed:

3. Click the Activity Monitor button.

A list of job activities appears:

File	Actions	View	Options	Windows					Help

Job ID	Job Type	Job State	Status	Class	Schedule	Client	Media Server
4920	Backup	Queued		silver1	incrbkps	silver	
4919	Backup	Active		silver2	incrbkps	silver	silver
4918	Backup	Active		silver2	incrbkps	silver	silver
4917	Backup	Done	0	silver1	incrbkps	silver	silver
4916	Backup	Done	0	shipyard_infx_db	shipyard_backup_policy	shipyard	shipyard
4915	Backup	Done	0	shipyard_infx_db	shipyard_backup_policy	shipyard	shipyard
4914	Backup	Done	0	shipyard_infx_db	shipyard_backup_policy	shipyard	shipyard
4913	Backup	Done	0	shipyard_infx_db	shipyard_backup_policy	shipyard	shipyard
4912	Backup	Done	0	shipyard_infx_db	shipyard_backup_policy	shipyard	shipyard
4911	Backup	Done	0	shipyard_infx_etc	shipyard_user_infx_etc	shipyard	shipyard
4910	Backup	Done	0	shipyard_infx_logs	shipyard_infx_logs_full	shipyard	shipyard
4909	Backup	Done	0	shipyard_infx_etc	shipyard_full_infx_etc	shipyard	shipyard
4908	Backup	Done	0	shipyard_infx_db	shipyard_full_db	shipyard	shipyard
4907	Backup	Done	0	steamer_store	incrbkps	steamer	bullet
4906	Backup	Done	0	steamer_os	incrbkps	steamer	bullet
4905	Backup	Done	0	steamer_AWS4	incrbkps	steamer	bullet
4904	Backup	Done	0	steamer_AWS3	incrbkps	steamer	bullet
4903	Backup	Done	0	steamer_AWS2	incrbkps	steamer	bullet

This list shows completed jobs, queued jobs, and active jobs.

For completed jobs, a status value of 0 indicates the job completed successfully. Any other status value needs to be investigated as it indicates job failure.

4. To sort the Activity Window different ways, select the View menu.

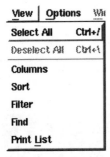

View	Options	Wi
Select All	**Ctrl+/**	
Deselect All	Ctrl+\	
Columns		
Sort		
Filter		
Find		
Print List		

Several options are available for displaying and categorizing jobs:

- Columns: Displays dialog box that enables rearranging of column display.

- Filter: Displays dialog box that enables criteria of jobs displayed to be modified.

■ Sort: Displays the sort window:

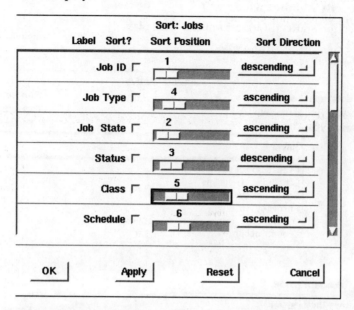

Moving the sliders changes priorities for the display. For example, moving Class to 1 automatically reorders the other sort criteria. Moving Class back to 5 resets it back. The display can be set to ascending or descending order.

5. **To obtain additional information about any job in the list, double click a job in the Activity Monitor window.**

   Detailed job status information is now displayed:

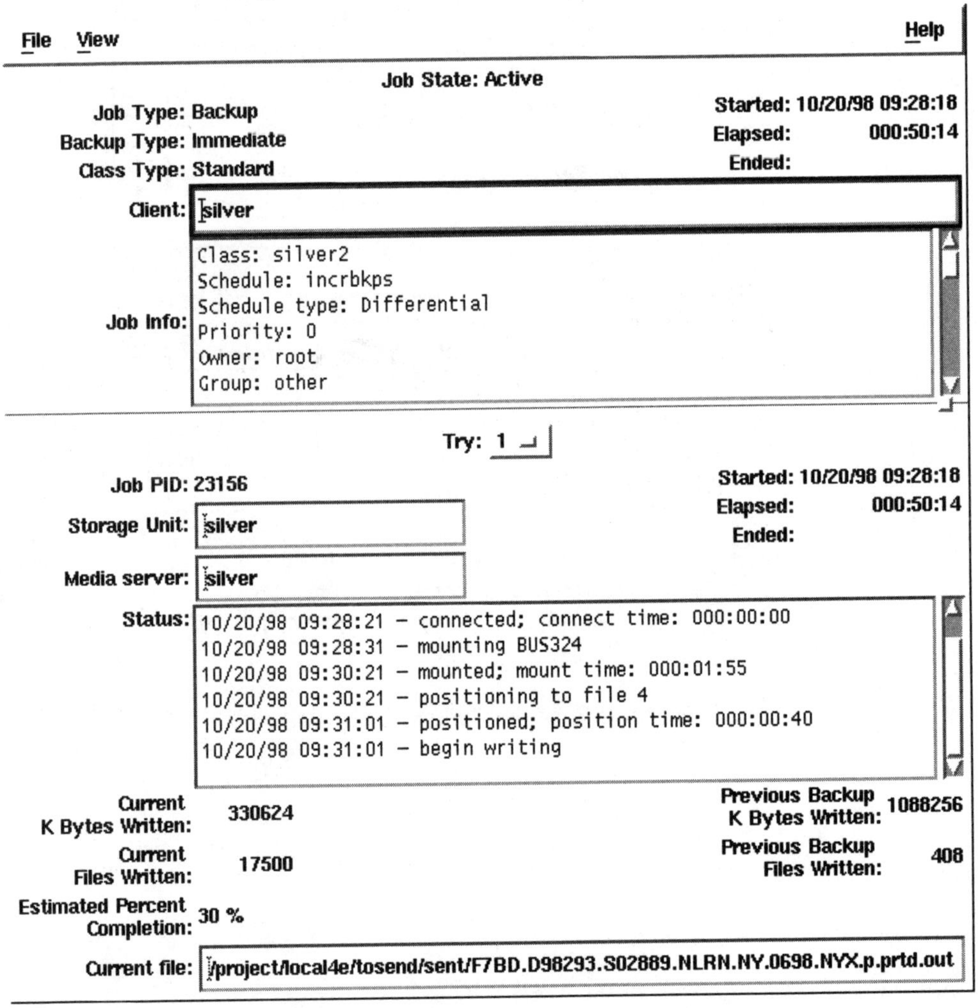
File
View
Help
Job State: Active
Job Type: Backup
Backup Type: Immediate
Class Type: Standard
Started: 10/20/98 09:28:18
Elapsed: 000:50:14
Ended:
Client: silver
Job Info:
Class: silver2
Schedule: incrbkps
Schedule type: Differential
Priority: 0
Owner: root
Group: other
Try: 1
Job PID: 23156
Storage Unit: silver
Media server: silver
Started: 10/20/98 09:28:18
Elapsed: 000:50:14
Ended:
Status:
10/20/98 09:28:21 - connected; connect time: 000:00:00
10/20/98 09:28:31 - mounting BUS324
10/20/98 09:30:21 - mounted; mount time: 000:01:55
10/20/98 09:30:21 - positioning to file 4
10/20/98 09:31:01 - positioned; position time: 000:00:40
10/20/98 09:31:01 - begin writing
Current K Bytes Written: 330624
Current Files Written: 17500
Previous Backup K Bytes Written: 1088256
Previous Backup Files Written: 408
Estimated Percent Completion: 30 %
Current file: /project/local4e/tosend/sent/F7BD.D98293.S02889.NLRN.NY.0698.NYX.p.prtd.out

Information displayed includes: job status, (in this case the job is active), time job was started, and length of time job has been running. A progress bar displays the percentage of estimated completion, along with the name of the file currently being backed up. This information is not displayed in real time; a new file name is displayed after each block of 500 files has been backed up. Information about number of bytes, and files backed up is also updated similarly.

▼ Killing Jobs

1. **Log in to the master Netbackup server as the system administrator.**

2. **Run this command:**

```
# /usr/openv/netbackup/bin/xnb -d display &
```

A GUI with the following buttons is displayed:

3. **Click the Activity Monitor button.**

A list of job activities is displayed:

File	Actions	View	Options	Windows				Help

Jobs — 1 of 113 selected

Job ID	Job Type	Job State	Status	Class	Schedule	Client	Media Server
4920	Backup	Queued		silver1	incrbkps	silver	
4919	Backup	Active		silver2	incrbkps	silver	silver
4918	Backup	Active		silver2	incrbkps	silver	silver
4917	Backup	Done	0	silver1	incrbkps	silver	silver
4916	Backup	Done	0	shipyard_infx_db	shipyard_backup_policy	shipyard	shipyard
4915	Backup	Done	0	shipyard_infx_db	shipyard_backup_policy	shipyard	shipyard
4914	Backup	Done	0	shipyard_infx_db	shipyard_backup_policy	shipyard	shipyard
4913	Backup	Done	0	shipyard_infx_db	shipyard_backup_policy	shipyard	shipyard
4912	Backup	Done	0	shipyard_infx_db	shipyard_backup_policy	shipyard	shipyard
4911	Backup	Done	0	shipyard_infx_etc	shipyard_user_infx_etc	shipyard	shipyard
4910	Backup	Done	0	shipyard_infx_logs	shipyard_infx_logs_full	shipyard	shipyard
4909	Backup	Done	0	shipyard_infx_etc	shipyard_full_infx_etc	shipyard	shipyard
4908	Backup	Done	0	shipyard_infx_db	shipyard_full_db	shipyard	shipyard
4907	Backup	Done	0	steamer_store	incrbkps	steamer	bullet
4906	Backup	Done	0	steamer_os	incrbkps	steamer	bullet
4905	Backup	Done	0	steamer_AWS4	incrbkps	steamer	bullet
4904	Backup	Done	0	steamer_AWS3	incrbkps	steamer	bullet
4903	Backup	Done	0	steamer_AWS2	incrbkps	steamer	bullet

4. To kill all jobs, click the `File` **menu and select** **K̲ill All Backups:**

File	Actions	View	Options	Windows			
Kill All Backups							
Refresh All		pe	Job State	Status	Class		
Exit			Active		silver1		
4919	Backup		Done	41	silver2		
4918	Backup		Done	150	silver2		

Note – This may take a few moments to execute and update the Status Window.

5. To kill an individual job, double click the job in the Activity Monitor.

Detailed job status information is displayed:

File	View		Help

Job State: Active

Job Type: **Backup**   Started: **10/20/98 09:28:18**
Backup Type: **Immediate**   Elapsed: **000:50:14**
Class Type: **Standard**   Ended:

Client: `silver`

Job Info:
```
Class: silver2
Schedule: incrbkps
Schedule type: Differential
Priority: 0
Owner: root
Group: other
```

Try: 1

Job PID: **23156**   Started: **10/20/98 09:28:18**
                                          Elapsed: **000:50:14**
Storage Unit: `silver`   Ended:

Media server: `silver`

Status:
```
10/20/98 09:28:21 — connected; connect time: 000:00:00
10/20/98 09:28:31 — mounting BUS324
10/20/98 09:30:21 — mounted; mount time: 000:01:55
10/20/98 09:30:21 — positioning to file 4
10/20/98 09:31:01 — positioned; position time: 000:00:40
10/20/98 09:31:01 — begin writing
```

Current K Bytes Written: **330624**   Previous Backup K Bytes Written: **1088256**

Current Files Written: **17500**   Previous Backup Files Written: **408**

Estimated Percent Completion: **30 %**

Current file: `/project/local4e/tosend/sent/F7BD.D98293.S02889.NLRN.NY.0698.NYX.p.prtd.out`

6. Click the `File` menu and select Kill.

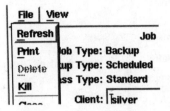

It may take a few moments to kill the job and update the Activity Monitor window.

NetBackup Reports

▼ Generating Reports

1. Log in to the master Netbackup server as the system administrator.

2. Run this command:

```
# /usr/openv/netbackup/bin/xnb -d display &
```

A GUI with the following buttons is displayed:

3. **Click the** Backup Management **button.**

The main xbpadmin window is displayed:

File	Actions	View	Options	Reports	Images	Windows	He

Classes

0 of 28 selec

Name	Type
bullet	Standard
clipper_AWS1	Standard
clipper_AWS2	Standard
clipper_AWS3	Standard
clipper_AWS4	Standard

Reports menu:
- Backup Status
- Client Backups
- Problems
- All Log Entries
- Media List
- Media Contents
- Images on Media
- Media Log Entries
- Media Summary
- Media Written
- ^ Implicit searching
- ✓ Explicit searching

Storage Units

0 of 6 selec

Name	NetBackup Host	Storage Type	robot number	Density
bullet1	bullet	Media		dlt
bullet2	bullet	Media		dlt
shipyard	shipyard	Media		dlt
silver	silver	Media Manager TLD		dlt

The Reports menu provides several report options. Selecting Backup Status (from menu on previous page) displays the following window:

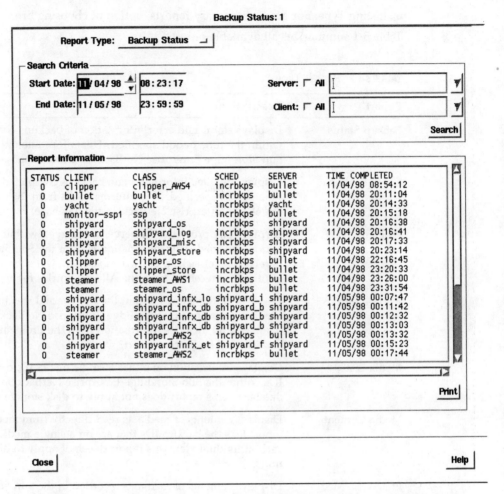

The Report Type box at the top of the window identifies the current report type being viewed. Other reports can be viewed by clicking this button and selecting from the drop down list.

4. **Depending on the report, the following can be specified in the** Search Criteria **section of the dialog box:**

- Start and End Date: Time period that report covers. The two main factors that determine length of time information is available are; the Duration to Retain Logs global attribute, and the retention period of the backup.

- Server: Server name and database that originated information.

- Client: Client name on the report.

- Volume Pool: For Media Summary reports, specifies volume pool.
- Media ID: For Media Reports, specifies media ID.
- Listing Type: For Media Summary reports, option of choosing brief or full view.

Table 5-1 summarizes all available reports.

TABLE 5-1   Report Types

Report	Description
Backup Status	Displays status and error information of backups completed within the time period specified. This information is from the Sun StoreEdge Enterprise NetBackUp error database.
Client Backups	Displays detailed information on backups completed within the time period specified. This information is from the Sun StoreEdge Enterprise NetBackUp file database.
Problems	Displays any problems the server has logged within the time period specified. This information is from the Sun StoreEdge Enterprise NetBackUp error database and is a subset of information received from the All Log Entries report.
All Log Entries	Displays all log entries within the time period specified. This report is from the Sun StoreEdge Enterprise NetBackUp error database and includes information from the Problems report, and Media Log Entries report.
Media List	Displays information on either a single media ID, or all media IDs within the Sun StoreEdge Enterprise NetBackUp media database. This report does not apply to disk storage units.
Media Contents	Displays contents of media as read directly from media. This report lists the backup IDs that are on a single media ID (not each individual file). This report does not apply to disk storage units.
Images on Media	Displays contents of media as recorded in the Sun StoreEdge Enterprise NetBackUp file database. This option can be used for any type of storage unit, including disk.

TABLE 5-1   Report Types

Report	Description
Media Log Entries	Displays media errors recorded in the Sun StoreEdge Enterprise NetBackUp error database. This information is a subset of information in the All Log Entries report.
Media Summary	Displays summary of active and nonactive media. Information is grouped according to expiration date. Shows expiration date of media and the number of media at each retention level.
Media Written	Displays removeable media used for backups within the time period specified. This report shows media used for image duplication (only if the original image was created prior to the time period specified).

5. **Before choosing a report, select either** Implicit Searching **or** Explicit Searching **from the** Reports **menu.**

With Implicit Searching (default), NetBackup produces a report based on information it finds within the time period specified by the Interval for Status Reports global attribute. In this mode, NetBackup will automatically generate a report as the selection is made from the Reports menu.

Implicit Searching applies only to Backup Status, Client Backups, Problems, and All Log Entries reports. Media reports are explicit regardless of whether explicit or implicit search mode is chosen.

With Explicit Searching, NetBackup uses the time period specified in the Search Criteria section of the report window. The report is run by clicking the Search button.

6. If the report is too large for viewing, access the file where the report is stored.

When a report is too large for viewing, a message is displayed at the top of the log file (Report Information window):

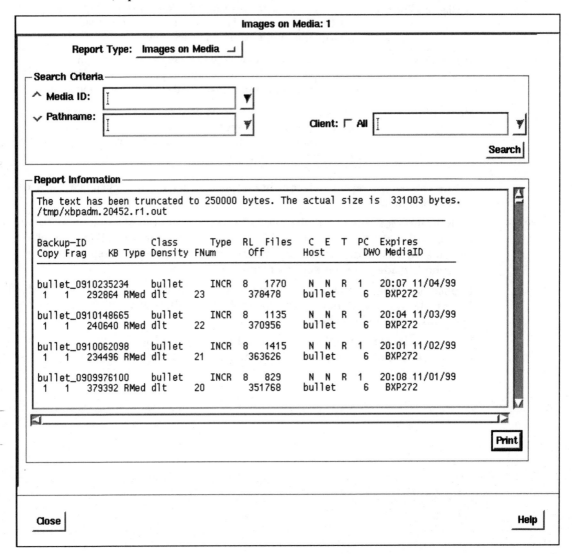

```
The text has been truncated to 250000 bytes. The actual size
is 331003 bytes. /tmp/xbpadm.20452.r1.out.
```

This message shows xbpadm has saved a copy in a temporary file. In this example, the file name is /tmp/xbpadm.17266.r2.out.

7. Print report.

Each window that has a Print button that enables the creation of a text file containing the report. When you click the Print button, the following a dialog box appears:

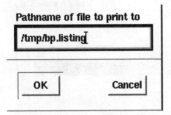

You can select the default directory (in this case /tmp), or select another directory as the location to save the report.

Manual Backup and Restore

▼ To Perform a Manual Backup

1. Log in to the master Netbackup server as the system administrator.

2. Run this command:

```
# /usr/openv/netbackup/bin/xnb -d display &
```

A GUI with the following buttons is displayed:

3. **Click the Backup Manager button.**

The main Backup Manager window is displayed.

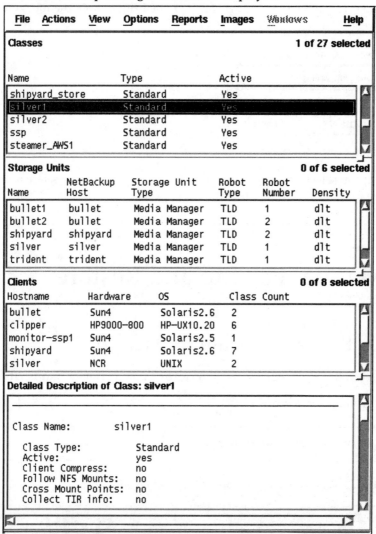

4. **In the** Classes **section, scroll the list until the required backup class is visible. Select the required class.**

5. Select the <u>A</u>ctions **menu and choose** <u>M</u>anual Backup:

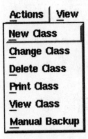

This Manual Backup window for the selected class is displayed:

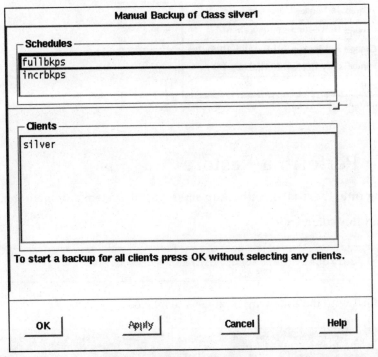

This window contains a client list and backup types (either full or incremental). Any client can be matched to either backup type. Full backup is the default.

6. Select OK or Apply to start the manual backup.

Note – Selecting OK closes the Manual Backup window; selecting Apply does not. Therefore, different types of jobs for different clients can be initiated using the Apply button.

---

7. **To verify the job has started, click the** File **menu and choose** Job Monitoring **(in either** Backup Manager **or** Activity Monitor **window):**

File	Actions	View	Options	Reports	Images	V
Job Monitor						
User Backup / Restore						
Media Management				Active		
Device Management				Yes		
Start NetBackup Daemons				Yes		
Log Request Daemon Status				Yes		
				Yes		
Re-Read Request Daemon Configuration				Yes		
Terminate Request Daemon						
Change NetBackup Configuration				Robot	Rol	
				Type	Nur	
Change NetBackup DB Backup Attributes				TLD	1	
Immediately Backup NetBackup DB ...				TLD	2	
Exit				TLD	2	
				TLD	1	
trident	trident	Media Manager		TLD	1	

▼ To Perform a Restore

1. **Log in to the master Netbackup server as the system administrator.**

2. **Run this command:**

```
# /usr/openv/netbackup/bin/xnb -d display &
```

A GUI with the following buttons is displayed:

3. Click the User Backup and Restore **button.**

The xbp main window is displayed:

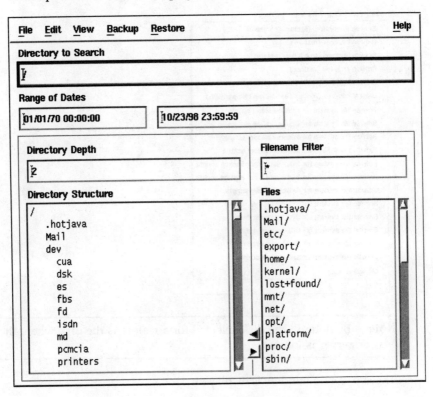

4. To restore a client or server other than the default, click the File menu and choose Configuration:

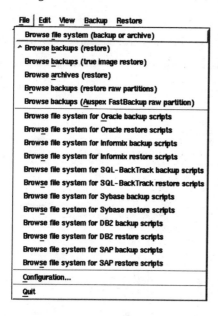

File	Edit	View	Backup	Restore

Browse file system (backup or archive)

^ Browse backups (restore)

Browse backups (true image restore)

Browse archives (restore)

Browse backups (restore raw partitions)

Browse backups (Auspex FastBackup raw partition)

Browse file system for Oracle backup scripts

Browse file system for Oracle restore scripts

Browse file system for Informix backup scripts

Browse file system for Informix restore scripts

Browse file system for SQL-BackTrack backup scripts

Browse file system for SQL-BackTrack restore scripts

Browse file system for Sybase backup scripts

Browse file system for Sybase restore scripts

Browse file system for DB2 backup scripts

Browse file system for DB2 restore scripts

Browse file system for SAP backup scripts

Browse file system for SAP restore scripts

Configuration...

Quit

Note – By default, the disk selected for a restore is the disk where the NetBackup Master Server is located.

The xbp_config window is displayed:

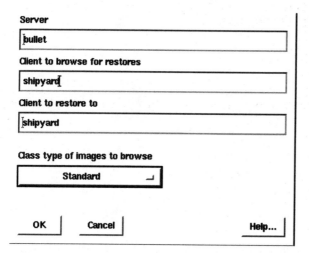

Server

bullet

Client to browse for restores

shipyard

Client to restore to

shipyard

Class type of images to browse

Standard

| OK | Cancel | Help... |

The name of the master server appears in the Server box. Initially, the master server name is set to the default master server for the client.

5. **To change the master server, follow these steps:**

   a. **Enter the name of the desired master server in the** Server **box.**

   b. **Click** OK.

   If an invalid name is entered, or the client selected does not belong to a NetBackup class on that server, one of the following error messages will be displayed:

   ```
   Could not connect to server
   Invalid client
   ```

6. **To restore files backed up by another client, follow these steps:**

   a. **Click the** File **menu and choose** Configuration.

   The xbp_config window is displayed.

   ```
   Server
   ┌─────────────────────────────────────────────┐
   │ bullet                                        │
   └─────────────────────────────────────────────┘
   Client to browse for restores
   ┌─────────────────────────────────────────────┐
   │ shipyard                                      │
   └─────────────────────────────────────────────┘
   Client to restore to
   ┌─────────────────────────────────────────────┐
   │ shipyard                                      │
   └─────────────────────────────────────────────┘

   Class type of images to browse
   ┌─────────────────────────────────┐
   │         Standard            ⌐|  │
   └─────────────────────────────────┘


      OK  │   Cancel  │              Help...  │
   ```

   b. **Enter the name of the client in the** Client to Browse for Restores **box.**

   c. **Click** OK.

   This enables the user to browse and restore files backed up by the client specified. However, the user must either be a system administrator for the master server or have the required permission.

   By default, the Client to Browse for Restores box displays the name of the client for the user session currently running.

   d. **In the** xbp **main window, click** Edit **menu and choose** Update Display.

7. **To direct a restore to another client, follow these steps:**

   a. **From the xbp main window, click the** File **menu and choose** Configuration.

      The xbp_config window is displayed.

   b. **Enter the name of the client in the** Client to Restore To **box.**

   c. **Click** OK.

   This enables the user to direct files to the client specified. However, the user must either be the system administrator for the master server or have the required permission.

   By default, the Client to Restore To box displays the name of the client for the user session currently running.

   d. **In the** xbp **main window, click the** Edit **menu and choose** Update Display.

8. **In the** xbp **main window, click the** File **menu and choose** Browse backups (restore). The Backup Images list opens in the main window and displays backup history for the client as stored on the NetBackup master server, for example:

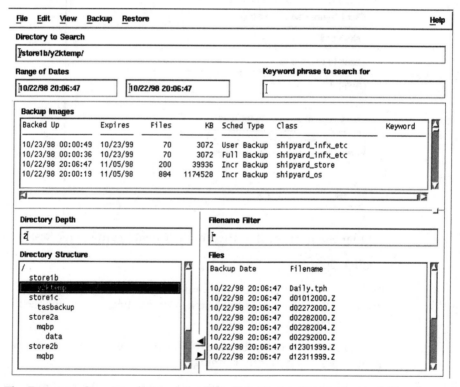

The Directory Structure list and the Files list display directories and files that match the criteria specified in previous steps.

If a large number of backup images match the specified Range of Dates, an error message informs the user that a specific path cannot be searched until the display is updated.

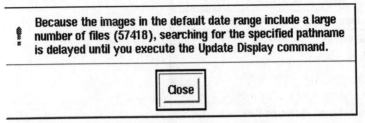

9. **If the previous error message is displayed; in the xbp main window, click Edit and choose Update Display:**

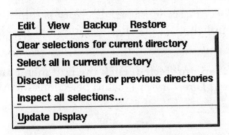

10. **Specify the** Directory to Search, Range of Dates, Keyword phrase to search for, Directory Depth, **and** Filename Filter **for files to restore.**

When changing from backup mode to restore mode, NetBackup defaults the starting date to the time of the last full backup. If a specific date is entered prior to switching modes, that date becomes the default.

If a client belongs to more than one class, the starting date defaults to the last full backup for whichever client was backed up first. For example, assume the client belongs to the shipyard_store class and shipyard_os class, and both classes receive full backups. If the last full backup for shipyard_store occurred before the last full backup for shipyard_os, then the window will display files ranging from the time of the shipyard_store backup.

If there are any links in the path being searched, by default NetBackup resolves the links so the path points to the actual file or directory. To stop any links being resolved, click the View menu and select Do Not Resolve Links in Search Directory. (Do this before choosing a browse command from the File menu.)

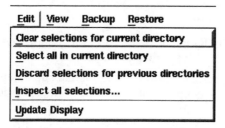

```
View │ Backup   Restore
┌─────────────────────────────────────────────┐
│ ▲ Brief display of filenames                 │
│   Verbose display of attributes and filenames│
│ ▲ Indented tree structure                    │
│   Full Pathnames                             │
│ ▲ All backup dates for each file             │
│   Only most recent backup date               │
│ ▲ Resolve Links in Search Directory          │
│   Do Not Resolve Links in Search Directory   │
└─────────────────────────────────────────────┘
```

11. **Find and select the files and directories to be restored.**

    In the previous example, the `/store1b/y2ktemp` directory is selected in the Directory Structure list. This implicitly selects all directories and files below `y2ktemp` in the directory tree.

12. **If a directory is selected and then unselected, click the** Edit **menu and choose either** Clear Selection for Current Directory **or** Discard Selections for All Directories.

```
Edit │ View   Backup   Restore
┌─────────────────────────────────────────────┐
│ Clear selections for current directory       │
│ Select all in current directory              │
│ Discard selections for previous directories  │
│ Inspect all selections...                    │
│ Update Display                               │
└─────────────────────────────────────────────┘
```

Note – Directories are not unselected until this action has been performed.

---

13. **To display the selection of items to be restored, click the Edit menu and choose**
Inspect all selections.

The following window is displayed.

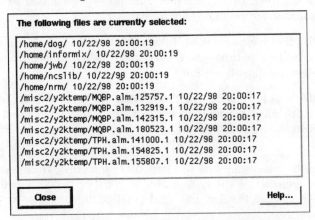

14. **To restore all selected files and directories to a path other than the one from which**
they were originally backed up, click the Restore menu and choose Specify
Alternate Pathname.

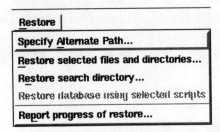

The xbp_altpath dialog box is displayed.

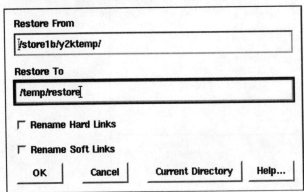

Only one alternate path can be specified, if the specified path does not exist,
NetBackup will create it when restoring the file.

15. **Enter the values in the** xbp_altpath **dialog box as follows.**

a. **Type the paths in the** Restore From **and** Restore To **text boxes**

   Alternatively, use the Current Directory button to set these paths to their default values, which is the current directory to search.

b. **To restore files that have specified links, click the** Rename Hard Links **button to rename the hard link pathnames. If the hard link pathnames should not be renamed, select the disable option**

c. **To restore files that have specified links, click the** Rename Soft Links **button to rename the soft link pathnames. If the soft link pathnames should not be renamed, select the disable option.**

Note – When restoring system files to a disk other than the current system disk, but plan to use the other disk as the system disk with the original file paths when the restore is completed, click the Rename Hard Links button and disable the Rename Soft Links button.

---

d. **Click** OK **to use specified settings during the next restore operation, or click** Cancel **to revert to the original settings.**

16. **To initiate a restore operation, click the** Restore **menu, and choose the appropriate restore command.**

   For example, if the Restore search directory is chosen, the xbp_confirm dialog box is displayed:

```
 OK to restore these files?
┌─────────────────────────────────────────────┐
│/export/home/ 10/24/98 20:05:44               │
│/etc/default/cron 10/24/98 20:05:44           │
│/etc/default/fs 10/24/98 20:05:44             │
│/etc/default/inetinit 10/24/98 20:05:44       │
│/etc/default/init 10/24/98 20:05:44           │
│/etc/default/kbd 10/24/98 20:05:44            │
│/etc/default/login 10/24/98 20:05:44          │
│/etc/default/passwd 10/24/98 20:05:44         │
│/etc/default/su 10/24/98 20:05:44             │
│/etc/default/sys-suspend 10/24/98 20:05:44    │
│/etc/default/tar 10/24/98 20:05:44            │
│/etc/default/utmpd 10/24/98 20:05:44          │
└─────────────────────────────────────────────┘

┌─────────────────┐
│ ⌐ Use log file  │
└─────────────────┘
Log filename
┌─────────────────────────────────────────────┐
│/bplog.rest.001                               │
└─────────────────────────────────────────────┘

 ⌐ Overwrite existing files

 ⌐ Restore to alternate path

 ⌐ Restore directories without crossing mount points

   OK  │    Cancel │                     Help... │
```

a. **Select the** Use log file **button to use the progress log file.**

If this button is enabled, a log file is created in the home directory. This file is updated as the operation progresses.

The name of the log file appears in the Log Filename text box.

b. **Select the** Overwrite existing files **button to overwrite files that have the same path names as the backed up files that are being restored.**

NetBackup restores files according to the original file pathname. The files are overwritten only if the file permissions allow it.

Note – The disk partition is overwritten regardless of how this option is set. The device file must exist.

---

c. **Select the** Restore to alternate path **button to restore to a previously specified alternate restore path.**

This button only appears if an alternate restore path was specified.

d. **Select the** Restore directories without crossing mount points **button to skip over file systems that are mounted beneath the selected directories.**

Note – The actual mount points beneath the selected directories will always be restored whether or not the *Restore directories without crossing mount points* button is selected. This button only affects the file systems beneath the mount points.

---

e. **Click** OK **to start the restore operation.**

▼ To Monitor a Restore

1. Log in to the master Netbackup server as the system administrator.

2. Run this command:

```
# /usr/openv/netbackup/bin/xnb -d display &
```

A GUI with the following buttons is displayed:

3. Click the User Backup and Restore **button.**

The main backup and restore window, known as xbp is displayed:

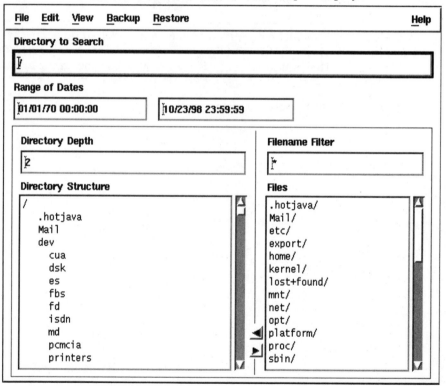

4. Click the **R**estore **menu and choose** Report progress of restore.

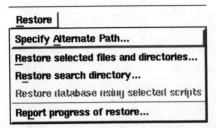

The Progress Report window is displayed.

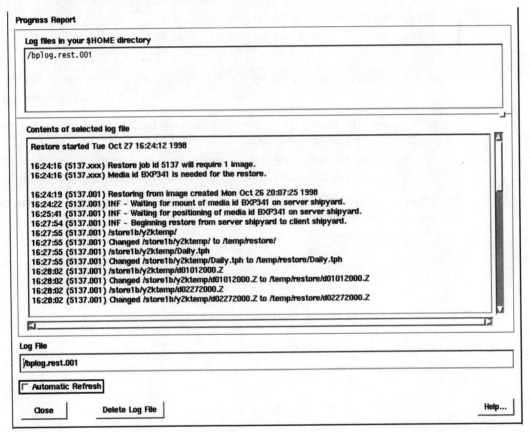

For any archive, backup, or restore operation, NetBackup creates a log file during the course of the operation. By default, this log file is created in the home directory, in one of the following forms:

- `bplog.bkup.`*n* for backup operations
- `bplog.arch.`*n* for archive operations
- `bplog.rest.`*n* for restore operations

Where *n* is a number unique to each file.

The Progress Report window lists the progress log files that reside in the home directory. (The log files can be viewed with a UNIX file editor by invoking the `more` or `tail` command.

The log information is displayed two lists:

- Log files in the `$HOME` directory, at the top of the window
- Contents of selected log files, in the middle section of the window

a. View the contents of a log by highlighting an entry in the upper list.

The list in the middle section displays entries NetBackup makes in the log file.

b. To change the rate at which NetBackup reads the file and updates the display, click one of the Automatic Refresh buttons:

- Select the Automatic Refresh button to enable automatic refreshes. A refresh of log file can be forced by reselecting the same file from the upper list.

5. When finished with monitoring the restore progress, click Close to return to the xbp_main window.

▼ To Delete Progress Log Files

1. **Log in to the master Netbackup server as the system administrator.**

2. **Run this command:**

```
# /usr/openv/netbackup/bin/xnb -d display &
```

A GUI with the following buttons is displayed:

3. **Click the** User Backup and Restore **button.**

The main backup and restore window, known as xbp is displayed:

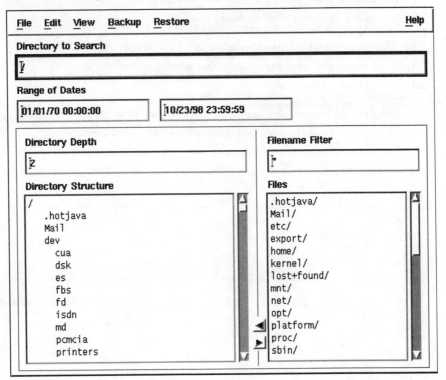

4. **Click the** <u>R</u>estore **menu and choose** Report progress of restore.

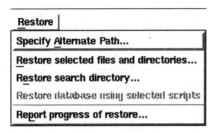

The Progress Report window is displayed.

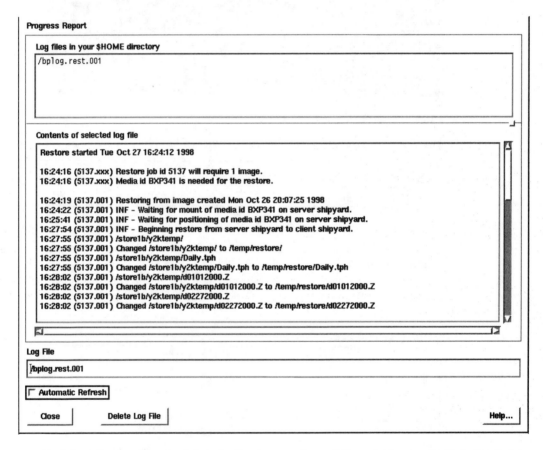

5. **Select the log files to delete in the top portion of the window, and click the** Delete Log File **button.**

Note – Log files can be deleted manually by using system commands. However, since log files can warn of problems, it is good practice to read log files before deleting them.

Interpreting Progress Logs

Progress log error messages notify the user of important events that occurred during a backup, restore, or archive operation. These messages have acronyms that specify the error level severity for an event.

Error level acronyms:

- INF—Informational message, no error occurred
- TRV—Trivial error message
- WRN—Warning error message
- ERR—Error message
- FTL—Fatal error message

Progress logs also list media requirements for any backup or restore. For backups, the progress log lists media IDs as NetBackup requests them during the course of the backup. For restores, the progress log begins by listing all media IDs that NetBackup needs to recover the backups containing the files. If a backup is split across more than one media ID, a restore log lists all media, however, NetBackup uses only what it needs to restore the requested files.

The results of any backup or restore can be determined by checking the status at the end of the log. If NetBackup was unable to backup or restore all requested files, check the exit status that appears a few lines before the end of the log. This status usually reveals the cause of the problem. An exit status of 0 means the operation was successful. Any nonzero exit status means the backup or restore operation was not entirely successful.

If the nonzero status code and any accompanying messages do not reveal the problem, check the *NetBackup Troubleshooting Guide*.

## CHAPTER 6

Oracle Parallel Export Script

Why a Parallel Export Script?

This chapter describes a script that performs fast Oracle database exports using Symmetric Multi Processing (SMP) machines. The performance benefit this script provides is nearly linear relative to the number of CPUs. For example, with 32 CPUs available for backups, a speed of nearly 32 times the standard database export can be achieved. Therefore, this script can be valuable for situations where exports of large amounts of mission-critical data need to be performed.

The script was contributed by its authors, Neal Sundberg and Mike Ellison from Qualcomm Inc. This approach was presented by Qualcomm in a paper called "Parallel Export/Import Today on SMP Machines" at the 1995 Oracle Users Week conference. The script continues to add value to Oracle's parallel features today. At Qualcomm, the IT staff routinely run this script on Sun Enterprise servers to perform an export of a 250 Gbyte database that takes approximately two hours. This task would be difficult to accomplish without using the parallel processing available on SMP machines.

The Oracle utilities for export and import are basically single-threaded processes that use a single CPU, with the exception of the *parallel query* feature. Under certain circumstances, the parallel query feature enables spawning of parallel processes that performs a SELECT operation against a large table. The degree of parallelism can be set for the table to the desired number of processes (such as four or eight). This parallel query feature takes advantage of multiple CPUs on an SMP machine, possibly breaking down the SELECT statement into separate smaller SELECT statements. However, it might not be desirable to apply parallelism to all tables since it could cause database problems.

Oracle provides features that support physical backup and restore, and logical backup and restore. The physical backup and restore features are the standard hot and cold backups, where a static image is taken of database files (although hot backups are not quite static). Basically, the database files are copied without really knowing what they contain. With this approach, if a disk drive is lost, or a controller writes some bad bytes to the database, a recovery can be made from the database point of view.

Export/import, on the other hand, takes the logical point of view. An export contains all the commands required to recreate the database, as if the commands were processed through the Oracle engine. For example, it includes commands such as CREATE DATABASE, ADD DATA FILES, and CREATE TABLE, as well as commands to add data to tables. Therefore, an export/import is similar to redoing the entire database by typing everything in by hand.

The export/import approach can be useful for disaster recovery or when migrating from one operating system to another. It also enables the logical restoration of part of a lost database. To restore one or two lost tables, the physical methodology cannot be used unless the tables are in their own table space, which is unlikely. However, there are cases where an export/import can be used to rebuild an entire system, or to defragment a database. This is probably the only way to do it without buying third-party tools.

The export/import approach can supplement a standard hot backup, and can be a lifesaver. For example, suppose your disk RAID and hot backup failed. In this situation, an available database export would serve as another layer of protection against failure in a system and would enable the recreation of the database. However, an export is only as good as the time it was taken as it is not possible to apply logs because of the system change numbers (SCNs).

Note – The SCNs help maintain consistency with the rest of the system. However, SCNs are specific to a particular instance of the database, therefore have no significance when rebuilding a database using the export/import utility.

Missing a days worth of transactions is better than having no data at all. However, it would not be advisable to keep database exports around for system failures, except as a third or fourth line of defense (depending on your configuration).

For example, suppose a new software program is released onto the system, and due to a lack of testing, the new program corrupts some tables in the database. In this case it would be desirable to have an export image to perform the imports against, and just restore the corrupted tables, thereby avoiding a rebuild of the entire database. There are other ways to recover from this situation, but the export/import method is probably the fastest. For example, the entire system on the test environment could be rebuilt, and brought up to the point in time just prior to the failure. By opening the test system and exporting the tables from there, the exports could be used to perform imports into the production system. However, this approach assumes that the test system can be down for the additional time it would take to implement the entire process.

Exports can be accomplished in either of two ways:

1. Database Running

Hot exports can be performed with the database up and running while transactions are being processed. This approach can be used to recover one table, or multiple tables. The backed up tables may be read-inconsistent with each other, therefore, some SQL *Plus re synchronization must be performed.

2. Database Down

The second way to perform an export, is to take the database down and put it into *restricted mode* (previously called DBA mode). Since all tables are consistent, the database can be completely restored from this export.

Qualcomm does not typically use exports for creation of a full database, or even as a recovery strategy.

A recovery strategy can be three layers deep:

- Highly Available Systems

The first layer of protection is from disk or hardware failure. This can be accomplished with a highly available system such as Sun™ Cluster and RAID.

- Hot Backup

The second layer of protection is an Oracle hot backup. This is a common method of putting the database into archive log mode, then backing up the archive logs between full backups. In this way, if media failure or physical system failure occurs, the entire database can be recovered from the full and incremental tape backups.

- Export

If there is a problem with the tape or data on it, an export can serve as a last line of defense.

Overview of the paresh Approach

The main script used to implement Oracle parallel exports is called paresh, for "PARallel Export SHell". The basic approach involves two steps:

1. **Structure Only Export**

   Perform a structure-only export of the entire database. This export includes objects such as tables, indexes, clusters, users, and accounts (at this point no data is exported). This step takes about 15 to 20 minutes depending on database size and hardware used. Build a list of database export commands based on this information. To perform this step, an approach such as the one described in the section "The list_tbls Script" on page 143can be used.

2. **Complete Data Export**

   Export all the data, one table at a time. There may be thousands of tables in a database. The paresh script keeps a specified number of table export processes running at any given time. The paresh script spawns processes for each of the export commands that were defined in the step above. The paresh script is described in further detail in the section "The paresh Script" on page 144.

   This approach uses a master process that spawns as many slaves as required. For example, if the level of parallelism is set to 10 processes, the paresh script takes the top 10 items in the task list produced by the list_tbls script, and spawns those 10 processes. As each process completes, the paresh script takes the next item from the list and spawns a new process for that item. In this way, 10 processes are kept running until the entire database export is completed. This makes optimal use of a backup server with 10 CPUs.

Note – The paresh script is basically a traffic cop for doing "parallel anything". A completely different set of tasks could be created other than those created by the list_tbls script, and still make use of the paresh script to spawn tasks in an optimal fashion.

The `list_tbls` Script

This SQL*Plus script is one example of how to create a file of commands that can be used by the `paresh` script. There are many different ways to accomplish the same task.

The `list_tbls.sql` script references the standard scripts `table_export.sh` and `full_export_no_rows.sh`.

The only parameter to `list_tbls.sql` is the name of the file to be used by the `paresh` script

CODE EXAMPLE 6-1   The `List_tbls` Script

```
whenever sqlerror exit sql.sqlcode;
set pause off;
set pages 0;
set linesize 132;
set feedback off;
set termout off;
column cmd_line format a80
column tick format a3
column sum_bytes format 999,999,999,999
! /bin/rm -f &&1;
spool &&1;
select './full_export_no_rows.sh' from dual;
select './table_export.sh '||owner||' '||segment_name cmd_line,
' # ' tick,
sum(bytes) sum_bytes
from dba_segments
where segment_type = 'TABLE'
and owner <> 'SYS'
group by owner, segment_name
order by sum(bytes) desc
;
spool off;
exit;
```

The `paresh` Script

This shell file controls multiple shell files in a parallel fashion. It uses two arguments, a file name, and the number of processes to run concurrently. The input file contains a list of all commands to be executed, along with their arguments. The number of parallel processes defaults to four, but can be set to any positive value.

The usage is:

```
# paresh commands_file parallel_count
```

where:

commands_file contains a list of commands or shell files to be executed. As all processing occurs in parallel, the execution order is not guaranteed. The commands are processed from the start of the list through to the end of the list.

parallel_count is the maximum number of slave processes spawned simultaneously

CODE EXAMPLE 6-2   The paresh Script

```
#! /bin/sh
#
#-------------------------------------------------------------
# message
#   Establish a timestamp and echo the message to the screen.
#   Tee the output (append) to a unique log file.
#-------------------------------------------------------------
#
message()
{
timestamp=`date +"%D %T"`
echo "$timestamp $*" | tee -a $logfile
return
}
```

```
#----------------------------------------------------------------
# get_shell
#   This function is responsible for establishing the next
#   command to be processed.  Since multiple processes might
#   be requesting a command at the same time, it has a built-
#   in locking mechanism.
#----------------------------------------------------------------
#
get_shell()
{
echo "`date` $1 Shell Request $$" >> $lklogfile
                                # debug locking file
while :                         # until a command or end
do
    next_shell=""               # initialize command
    if [ ! -s ${workfile} ]     # if empty file (end)
    then                        #
    break                       # no more commands
    fi                          #
    if [ ! -f $lockfile ]       # is there a lock?
    then                        # not yet...
    echo $$ > $lockfile         # make one
    echo "`date` $1 Lock Obtained $$" >> $lklogfile
                                #debug
    if [ "$$" = "`cat $lockfile`" ]
                                # double check that
    then                        # we created it last
       next_shell=`sed -e q $workfile`
                                # first line of file
        sed -e 1d $workfile > ${workfile}.tmp    # Chop 1st line
        mv ${workfile}.tmp $workfile
                                # rename to work file
        rm -f $lockfile         # turn off lock
        echo "`date` $1 Shell Issued " >> $lklogfile    #debug
        return                  # done, command in
        else                    # variable "next_shell"
        echo "`date` $1 Lock FAULTED $$" >> $lklogfile  # debug
        fi                      # double check faulted
#       else                    # locked by other
#       echo "`date` $1 Lock Wait $$" >> $lklogfile # debug
        fi                      #
        sleep 1                 # brief pause
done                            # try again
return                          # only if no commands
}
```

```
#----------------------------------------------------------------
# paresh_slave
#    This code is executed by each of the slaves. It basically
#    requests a command, executes it, and returns the status.
#----------------------------------------------------------------
#
paresh_slave()
{
shell_count=0                   # Commands done by this slave
get_shell $1                    # get next command to execute
while test "$next_shell" != ""
                                # if no command, all done
do                              # got a command
    shell_count=`expr $shell_count + 1`
                                # increment counter
    message "Slave $1: Running  Shell $next_shell"
                                # message
    $next_shell                 # execute command
    shell_status=$?             # get exit status
    if [ "$shell_status" -gt 0 ]
                                # on error
    then                        # then message
    message "Slave $1: ERROR IN Shell $next_shell
status=$shell_status"
    echo "Slave $1: ERROR IN Shell $next_shell
status=$shell_status" >> $errfile
    fi                          #
#   message "Slave $1: Finished Shell $next_shell"
                                # message
    get_shell $1                # get next command
done                            # all done
message "Slave $1: Done (Executed $shell_count Shells)"
                                # message
return                          # slave complete
}
```

```
# paresh_driver
#   This code is executed by the top level process only. It
#   parses the arguments and spawns the appropriate number
#   of slaves.  Note that the slaves run this same shell file,
#   but the slaves execute different code, based on the
#   exported variable PARESH.
#-------------------------------------------------------------
#
paresh_driver()
{
rm -f $lklogfile                    # start a new log file
if [ "$1" = "" ]                    # first argument?
then                                # no?
    master_file="master.list"       # default value
else                                # yes?
    if [ ! -f "$1" ]                # does file exist?
    then                            # no?
    echo "$0: Unable to find File $1"
                                    # say so
    exit 1                          # quit
    else                            # yes?
    master_file="$1"                # use specified filename
    fi
fi
if [ "$2" = "" ]                    # Second Argument?
then                                # no?
    parallel_count=4# default value
else                                # Yes?
    if [ "$2" -lt 1 ]               # Less than 1?
    then                            # Yes?
    echo "$0: Parallel Process Count Must be > 0"
                                    # message
    exit 1                          # quit
    else                            # no?
    parallel_count=$2               # Use Specified Count
    fi
fi
```

```
message "-------------------------------"      # Startup Banner
message "Master Process ID:  $PARESH"
message "Processing File:    $master_file"
message "Parallel Count:     $parallel_count"
message "Log File:           $logfile"
message "-------------------------------"
cp $master_file $workfile          # make a copy of commands file
while test  $parallel_count -gt 0 # Have we started all slaves?
do                                 # Not yet
    if [ ! -s $workfile ]          # Is there work to do?
    then                           # No?
    message "All Work Completed - Stopped Spawning at
$parallel_count"
    break                          # Quit spawning
    fi
    $0 $parallel_count &# spawn a slave (with slave #)
    message "Spawned Slave $parallel_count  [pid $!]"
                                   # message
    parallel_count=`expr $parallel_count - 1`
                                   # decrement counter
done                               # Next
wait                               # Wait for all slaves
message "All Done"                 # message
return                             # Function Complete
}
```

```
#-------------------------------------------------------------
# main
#   This is the main section of the program. Because this shell
#   file calls itself, it uses a variable to establish whether or
#   not it is in Driver Mode or Slave Mode.
#-------------------------------------------------------------
#
if [ "$PARESH" != "" ]# If variable is set
then                                    # then slave mode
    workfile=/tmp/paresh.work.$PARESH # Work file with parent pid
    lockfile=/tmp/paresh.lock.$PARESH # Lock file with parent pid
    lklogfile=/tmp/paresh.lklog.$PARESH
                                        # LockLog file with
                                        # parent pid
    logfile=/tmp/paresh.log.$PARESH   # Log File with parent pid
    errfile=/tmp/paresh.err.$PARESH   # Error File with parent pid
    paresh_slave $*                    # Execute Slave Code
else                                    #
    PARESH="$$"; export PARESH         # Establish Parent pid
    workfile=/tmp/paresh.work.$PARESH # Work File with parent pid
    lockfile=/tmp/paresh.lock.$PARESH # Lock File with parent pid
    lklogfile=/tmp/paresh.lklog.$PARESH
                                        # LockLog File with
                                        # parent pid
    logfile=/tmp/paresh.log.$PARESH   # Log File with parent pid
    errfile=/tmp/paresh.err.$PARESH   # Error File with parent pid
    rm -f $errfile                     # remove error file
    paresh_driver $*                   # execute Driver Code
    rm -f $workfile                    # remove work file
    rm -f $lklogfile                   # remove lock log file
    if [ -f $errfile ]                 # Is there was an error
    then
    message "**************************************************"
    message "FINAL ERROR SUMMARY. Errors logged in $errfile"
    cat $errfile | tee -a $logfile
    message "**************************************************"
    exit 1
    fi
fi
exit
```

High-Speed Database Backups on Sun Systems

Executive Summary

Overview

As multi-Tbyte databases become common, and available backup windows continue to shrink, the issue of backing up very large databases in the shortest possible time has become increasingly urgent. To address this problem, Sun Microsystems, Inc., VERITAS Software Corp., the Oracle Corp., and Storage Technology Corp. (STK) came together in the Sun Enterprise Technology Center to conduct high-speed database backup scalability tests. The three scenarios tested were:

1. **Online, or hot backup of an Oracle database**

2. **Offline, or cold backup of an Oracle database**

3. **Raw device backup of the Oracle database volumes.**

Results

The testing achieved record-breaking results, demonstrating enterprise-level backup requirements for mission-critical databases can be met in open systems environments. The final results were:

- Hot backup of an Oracle7 database at a sustained rate of 941 Gbyte/hr.
- Cold backup of an Oracle7 database at a sustained rate of 940 Gbyte/hr.
- Raw device backup of Oracle7 database volumes at a sustained rate of 1026 Gbyte/hr.

Note – These tests were conducted approximately three years ago at the time of this writing. Faster backup rates could be achieved with tests run today.

Conclusion

These results demonstrate high speed backups of large databases are possible with the technology available from Sun, VERITAS NetBackup, Oracle, and STK products. The ability to backup a live Oracle database at nearly one Tbyte/hr. means the backing up of multi-Tbyte databases can now be accomplished in a few hours while still allowing the user continuous access to data. Raw volume being backed up at greater than one Tbyte/hr. demonstrates that backing up raw devices is a viable backup strategy in some environments.

Technology for High Performance Backups

To evaluate the effectiveness of online, offline, and raw database backups using the latest software and hardware technologies, Sun called upon their internal benchmarking center. The Sun Enterprise Technology Center provides a permanent, multi system facility that serves as a proving ground for scalability and reliability of Sun Microsystems products in large-scale enterprise environments.

Hardware Configuration

The Sun Enterprise Technology Center configured a Sun Enterprise 6000 server with more than one Tbyte of high performance disk storage and 24 of the fastest tape drives available (at the time of this test). For raw device backups, Sun installed an additional five Sun StorEdge DLT 7000 tape drives to increase I/O throughput. The Sun Enterprise 6000 server was configured with twelve 250 MHz CPUs on six processor boards which hosted a total of 2 Gbytes of RAM. The I/O configuration supported 17 SPARCstorage Arrays and 24 StorageTek RedWood SD-3 tape drives. The remaining ten slots on the Sun Enterprise 6000 server were populated with I/O cards and interfaces for the disk and tape drives.

Each of the SD-3 tape drives were connected to the server via a separate S-Bus based Differential Wide SCSI interface. Differential Wide SCSI was the choice for this configuration as it supported the long cable lengths required for an installation of this size. The SD-3 drives, as well as the additional DLT 7000 drives, were used in compressed mode, with a compression factor of 1.4 for moving data to the tape.

Each of the 17 SPARCstorage Array Model 112 systems were configured with 30 disk drives, each 2.1 Gbytes in size, totalling more than one Tbyte of storage. The SPARCstorage Arrays were connected to the Sun Enterprise 6000 I/O cards via dual Fibre Channel interfaces supported by the card. The arrays were configured with mirroring and striping, allowing half a Tbyte available for database configuration.

Software Configuration

The Sun Enterprise Technology Center configured the server with the highest-performance database backup software currently available. Each software component was used without modification, thereby demonstrating off-the-shelf products can be used to achieve high database backup rates:

- Solaris Operating Environment, Version 2.5.1

    Support for each software package begins with the Solaris operating environment. Because the Solaris operating environment is multi-threaded, many processors working in parallel are used to accelerate operations such as I/O. High-performance databases such as Oracle use process-level threading to run many operations in parallel, thereby increasing transaction rates. In this test, the ability to use all 14 processors for both database and backup operations was essential.

- Sun StorEdge Volume Manager, Version 2.3

    The Solaris operating environment was enhanced with the Sun StorEdge Volume Manager, which was used to configure data striping and mirroring on the SPARCstorage Array, and to aggregate many physical drives into a smaller collection of logical volumes.

- Oracle Version 7.3.3

    The database management system chosen for the test was Oracle 7.3.3. The database was populated with a generic mix of records similar to those found in any large decision support system database. The database was configured with ten tablespaces, using 79 data files, each 4 Gbytes in size.

- Oracle Enterprise Backup Utility (EBU), Version 2.1 Beta

    The Oracle EBU provides a set of application programming interfaces for controlling database operations, and for providing parallel backup streams to tape storage management software. EBU was used to control database operations to ensure a consistent image of the database would be available for backup operations. A software patch from Oracle was applied to EBU.

- VERITAS NetBackup, Version 2.1

    The NetBackup software, with its Database Extension, handled data movement between Oracle EBU and the StorageTek RedWood tape units. Since NetBackup manages volume labels, there is no confusion about which tape cartridge contains specific data. For this reason, NetBackup was used to manage the raw disk backups as well as online and offline database backups through Oracle EBU. One of the features of NetBackup is the ability to multiplex parallel backup streams onto a single volume. To transfer the 79 data files with the maximum amount of parallelism, NetBackup was configured to multiplex three to four datafiles into each stream of data stored to tape. A software patch from VERITAS was applied to this version of the NetBackup software.

Delivering High-Speed Database Backups

Sun measured backup throughput for online, offline, and raw disk backups. The most notable feature occurred during the portion of the backup process when NetBackup streamed data from all devices in parallel, the configuration sustained raw disk backup rates of more than one Tbyte/hr.

For online and offline backups, sustained rates of approximately 940 Gbyte/hr. were achieved, with no significant difference between the online and offline backups.

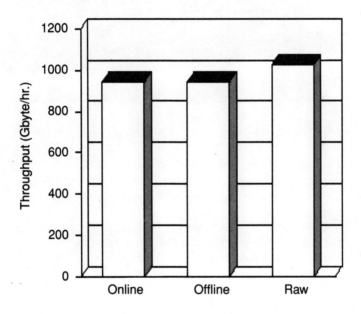

FIGURE A-1 Sustained rates of throughput for parallel backup of online, offline, and raw disk backups.

A graph of throughput over time for online, offline, and raw disk backups is shown in FIGURE A-2

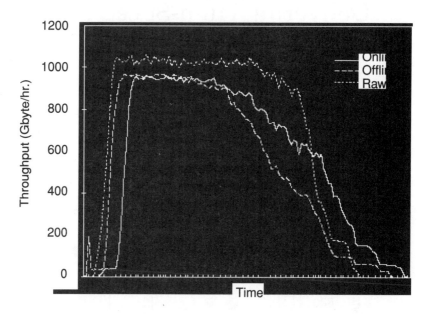

FIGURE A-2   Throughput over time for on-line, off-line, and raw disk backups

- During the *start-up phase*, EBU and NetBackup required time to calculate the data to be backed up. The least amount of time required was for the raw backup, where only the raw disk partitions were inventoried. More time was required to start up offline backups because of the additional overhead in calculating the logical structures to be transferred to NetBackup. The longest start-up time was for online backups, where the database was put into archive log mode, thereby ensuring a consistent database state and setup for transactions to be logged rather than committed to the actual tablespaces. There was no concurrent transaction load during online tests.

- During the *parallel phase*, NetBackup transferred multiplexed streams of three to four datafiles or raw disk partitions to each of the 24 RedWood backup devices. (For raw disk backups, an additional five DLT 7000 tape drives were used) This period was dominated by high-speed data transfer. The plateaus of the throughput curves illustrated in Figure A-2 show sustained rates of 1026 Gbyte/hr. for raw backups and approximately 940 Gbyte/hr. for the online and offline backups.

It is important to note that the database used in this test was of average size for an OLTP configuration, but is small in comparison to many databases in use today. With decision support systems and data warehouses sized at one Tbyte and larger, Sun expects the parallel phase to dominate the backup process. This means customers with large databases can realize sustained backup speeds of around 940 Gbytes to one Tbyte/hr.

- During the *ramp-down phase*, throughput drops off gradually rather than suddenly because datafiles and disk partitions are not equally-sized, and therefore do not all complete at once. Finally, during the ramp-down phase, NetBackup completes its bookkeeping and the last portion of the data is written to the tape devices.

TABLE A-1   Summary of performance statistics for online, offline, and raw device backups

Benchmark	Sustained Parallel Throughput	Total Data Moved	Time for Test	Overall Average Throughput	CPU Utilization
Online backup	941 Gbyte/hr.	271 GB	30 min	580 Gbyte/hr.	62%
Offline backup	940 Gbyte/hr.	271 GB	27 min	640 Gbyte/hr.	60%
Raw backup	1026 Gbyte/hr.	291 GB	21 min	831 Gbyte/hr.	50%

The overall results demonstrate that, whether the database is large or small, extremely high rates of I/O throughput are available.

Highlights of testing:

- For the online backup, a total of 271 Gbytes was transferred to tape in 30 minutes, achieving an overall average throughput of 580 Gbyte/hr. For this, as well as the offline and raw tests, the tape drives were configured in compressed mode, with a compression ratio of 1.4:1 observed for the data used in this test. On a per-drive basis, this configuration yielded a sustained parallel throughput of over 39 Gbyte/hr.

- The offline backup moved the same amount of data in 27 minutes, delivering an average throughput of 640 Gbyte/hr. As with the online backup, a sustained parallel throughput per drive was more than 39 Gbyte/hr.

- The raw disk backup completed in the least amount of time, even considering that using the raw devices required more data (291 Gbytes) to be moved. The raw disk backup was achieved in 21 minutes and had an average throughput rate of 831 Gbyte/hr. This test used 24 RedWood SD-3 tape drives and the additional Sun DLT 7000 drives. The RedWood drives achieved almost 39 Gbyte/hr. throughput per drive, with the DLT 7000 drives contributing a maximum of 22.8 Gbyte/hr. each.

With high-performance servers such as the Sun Enterprise 6000, the resource demands made on the CPU for backups still left additional room for other activities. CPU usage for these tests was relatively low, being: 62% for online, 60% for offline, and 50% for raw backups. These numbers indicate average use over the twelve CPUs.

The low CPU usage observed during the tests indicate the Sun Enterprise 6000 server has the capacity to scale to higher throughput levels. Indeed, with only 50 percent of the twelve CPUs used to achieve more than one Tbyte/hr. throughput to tape, Sun discovered the limiting factor was disk I/O throughput. If a greater number of disk spindles or faster devices were available to increase disk I/O bandwidth, the next bottleneck would be the total throughput available from the tape drives. These tests established that even at one Tbyte/hr. backup rate, the tests did not reach the scalability limit of the Sun Enterprise 6000 server. This demonstrates that Sun customers are able to backup their databases as fast as they wish, provided they are willing to invest in disk and tape capacity to do so.

A Range of Backup Solutions

The days when only mainframes could sustain the backup rates needed to support enterprise-critical database backups are over. With scalable and configureable database servers, storage management software from Sun and VERITAS, state-of-the-art tape backup systems from StorageTek, and superior database management software from Oracle, impressive rates in backup throughput can be achieved. Raw disk backup rates in excess of one Tbyte/hr. give rise to new strategies for very large database backups. Backups of multi-Tbyte databases can now be accomplished in a few hours, allowing IT organizations to provide continuous access to data while safely securing the data critical to success in today's competitive marketplace.

Sun realizes that not every IT organization has multi-Tbyte databases, and that not all backup requirements are so critical as to require the support of two dozen of the world's best backup systems. Sun offers a wide range of scalable database servers, and a variety of choices for low-cost tape backup systems. The company's flexible database servers have CPU performance and I/O throughput that can be balanced specifically for any situation.

Business Continuity Planning and Sun Technologies

Introduction

Business continuity planning will be addressed in detail in the forthcoming Sun BluePrint book *Business Continuity Planning*. Since this topic is closely related to backup and restore issues, this appendix has been added. It provides an overview of business continuity issues and Sun technologies.

Planning for Continuity

Data and communication centers are the heart of most companies today. When either key asset is compromised—whether by hardware failure, software failure, data corruption, or data loss—a company may face potentially severe losses unless a robust contingency plan is in place.

An enterprise-wide contingency plan can provide many benefits. Perhaps the most important, direct, and measurable benefit of such a strategy is that it will minimize financial losses in the face of disaster. Having a solid, well-tested plan will help restore IT and telecommunications infrastructures quickly, and minimize interruptions for personnel, suppliers, vendors, partners, investors, and customers. Fast restoration will strengthen the company's reputation and professional standing in the business community.

Business Continuity Planning

The process of creating, testing, and maintaining an organization-wide plan to recover from any form of disaster is called Business Continuity Planning. Every BCP strategy includes three fundamental components:

- Risk assessment.
- Contingency planning.
- Disaster recovery process.

BCP should encompass every type of business interruption—from a minor short-lived power outage or spike, up to the worst possible natural disaster or terrorist attack.

Sun and BCP

To help plan against potential disasters, Sun provides an array of products, services, and alliances which can form a core component of your Business Continuity Plan.

Sun Enterprise Clusters Solutions

Sun Cluster systems and software provides high availability and fast recovery for critical data and services. Sun Cluster software reduces the downtime risk by quickly restoring system services after a hardware or software fault. The Sun Cluster has been designed for maximum system continuity by delivering high availability through fault detection—and is capable of automatically detecting system failure and redirecting all processing to a backup system quickly and transparently.

This capability significantly lowers recovery time and thereby reduces costs.

Dynamic System Domains

Dynamic System Domains bring mainframe-style partitioning capabilities to the UNIX world. These domains allow a single Sun Enterprise 10000 platform to be logically divided into multiple or "stand-alone" servers. Every Dynamic System Domain remains logically isolated from other domains within the system. Most sites require separate environments for development, testing, and production.

Since domains allow multiple applications to run in isolation on a single server, they play an important role in consolidation and business continuity planning as they reduce the number of platforms that must be managed.

Sun StorEdge™ Instant Image

Instant Image is a point-in-time copy facility that keeps data available, thereby enhancing business continuity. Instant Image takes snapshots of live data for decision support, contingency planning, and revision control without disrupting online transactions. This product creates a "shadow" image of the data that can be read from or written to, just like the original. This helps keep business applications up and running while performing backups, loading data warehouses, or migrating data by using a point-in-time snapshot. Applications can be developed and tested using actual production data. Instant Image also tracks any differences between the master data and copy—making data resynchronization fast and easy.

Sun StorEdge™ L700 Tape Library

The Sun StorEdge L700 Tape Library is the highest capacity, most highly available tape library, and has been designed to support the backup and recovery needs of datacenter customers running data-intensive applications in mission-critical environments. The library offers approximately 14 Tbytes of capacity, making it the ideal backup solution for massive file systems such as those commonly found in large databases, data warehouses, enterprise servers, and datacenters. Additional features include hot-pluggable and redundant components that support RAS capabilities, including drives, fans, and power supplies.

Sun Data Center Consolidation Program

The Sun Data Center Consolidation Program helps companies reduce IT complexity and lower the total cost of ownership and IT infrastructure by physically consolidating servers, and logically consolidating applications. Sun will evaluate a customers existing infrastructure and identify areas where major benefits from consolidation could be realized. Sun provides professional installation, system migration, testing, and support services necessary for a smooth, uninterrupted consolidation transition.

Continuity Alliances

Sun Professional Services will work with a customer's preferred disaster recovery vendor to provide a tailored plan to suit the customer's business, recovery, and budget requirements. Sun Business Continuity Management Services (a division of Sun Professional Services) works closely with world-class continuity vendors—such as Comdisco, Computer Site Engineering, Guardian iT, IBM Corp., and SunGard Recovery Services Inc. to provide a customized, optimized strategy for business continuity and disaster recovery.

Glossary

archive logs	Oracle database files used to bring data files up-to-date while the database is online or offline. Archive logs help to restore the database to a specific point in time.
Asynchronous Transfer Mode (ATM)	A standard for switching and routing all types of digital information, including video, voice, and data. With ATM, digital information is broken down into standard-sized packets, each with the "address" of its final destination.
ATL	A tape library vendor. The company's full name is ATL Products.
ATM	See *Asynchronous Transfer Mode*
Automatic Multistreaming	A feature of NetBackup. If a server is attached to several disk drives, and the "all local drives" selection is made, data will be backed up as separate streams. With this selection specified, the data automatically streams to either multiple tape drives, or a single tape drive.
atomicity	An operation that can never be interrupted or left in an incomplete state under any circumstance.
backup	A copy on a diskette, tape, or disk of some or all of the files from a hard disk. There are two types of backups: a full backup and an incremental backup. Synonymous with "dump".
backup schedule	The scheduled times when automatic backups will occur.
backup server	A server that runs backup software, such as NetBackup or Solstice Backup, and performs backup operations. The data to be backed up may also reside on the backup server as well as on other servers.
block-level incremental backups	A feature of both NetBackup and Solstice Backup that makes it possible to backup only blocks modified since the most recent backup.
BMC PATROL	A product suite for application management from BMC Software, Inc.

bus	(1) A circuit over which data or power is transmitted, that often acts as a common connection among a number of locations. (2) A set of parallel communication lines that connect major components of a computer system, including CPU, memory, and device controllers.
cache	A buffer of high-speed memory filled at medium speed from main memory, often with instructions. A cache increases effective memory transfer rates and processor speed.
CLI	Command line interface.
cold database backup	The process of backing up a database that is offline (not actively supporting transactions).
database management System (DBMS)	A software system for database creation and maintenance and execution of programs using the database.
demultiplexing	The process of extracting and saving *individual* backup images from one or more tapes that contain *multiple* backup images resulting from a multiplexed backup.
direct I/O	A method of accessing files in a filesystem as though they were raw devices.
EBU	Oracle's Enterprise Backup Utility, a high performance interface for backing up Oracle databases. Sometimes referred to as OEBU (for Oracle Enterprise Backup Utility). The Oracle Recovery Manager (RMAN) is the Oracle8 equivalent of EBU.
ERP	Enterprise resource planning.
Ethernet	A type of local area network that enables real-time communication between machines connected directly together through cables. Ethernet was originally developed by Xerox in 1976, for linking minicomputers at the Palo Alto Research Center. A widely implemented network from which the IEEE 802.3 standard for contention networks was developed, Ethernet uses a bus topology (configuration) and relies on the form of access known as CSMA/CD to regulate traffic on the main communication line. Network nodes are connected by coaxial cable (with two variations), or by twisted-pair wiring.
Exabyte Corp.	A supplier of tape storage and automation solutions for the data-intensive application and database server markets.
export	The process of writing data from an Oracle database into a transportable operating system file. An *import* reads data from this file back into an Oracle database.
FC-AL	See *Fiber Channel Arbitrated Loop*

FDDI	Fiber distributed data interface. A high-speed networking standard. The underlying medium is fiber optics, and the topology is a dual-attached, counter-rotating token ring. FDDI networks can be identified by the orange fiber "cable".
Fiber Channel Arbitrated Loop (FC-AL)	A high bandwidth, serial communication technology which supports 100 Mbyte/sec. per loop. Most systems support dual loop connections which provides a total bandwidth of 200 Mbyte/sec.
filesystem	See *UNIX filesystem*
FlashBackup	A feature of NetBackup that performs fast backups of an entire raw partition, bypassing the filesystem. However, inode information is tracked, so individual files can be restored.
full dump	A copy of the contents of a file system backed up for archival purposes. Contrast with *incremental dump*.
GDM	See *Global Data Master*
Genesys	A program, consisting of products and services, aimed at helping IT organizations dot com their datacenters.
Gigabit Ethernet	A networking technology that provides 1 Gbit/sec. bandwidth for campus networks based on the simplicity of Ethernet at a lower cost than other technologies of comparable speed.
Gbyte	One billion bytes. In reference to computers, bytes are often expressed in multiples of powers of two. Therefore, a Gbyte can also be 1024 Mbyte, where a Mbyte is considered to be 2^20 (or 1,048,576) bytes.
Global Data Master (GDM)	A VERITAS product that extends NetBackup centralized management to global WAN environments. The NetBackup Global Data Manager overlays existing NetBackup environments and provides single-point-administration for a group of widely distributed NetBackup servers.
hot database backup	The backup of an active database (currently supporting transactions).
import	The process of reading data from an operating system file into an Oracle database. The operating system file is originally created by performing an *export* on the database.
incremental dump	A duplicate copy of files that have changed since a certain date. An incremental dump is used for archival purposes. Contrast with *full dump*.
internet	A collection of networks interconnected by a set of routers that enable them to function as a single, large virtual network.

I/O	Input/output. Refers to equipment used to communicate with a computer, the data involved in the communication, the media carrying the data, and the process of communicating the information.
interprocess control (IPC)	The process of sharing data between processes, and coordinating access to the shared data.
kernel	The core of the operating system software. The kernel manages the hardware (for example, processor cycles and memory) and enables fundamental services such as filing.
local area network (LAN)	A group of computer systems in close proximity that can communicate with one another via connecting hardware and software.
Legato Networker	A backup tool from Legato Systems, Inc. Sun distributes an OEM version of this product under the name Solstice Backup.
library	See *tape library*
local host	The CPU or computer on which a software application is running; the workstation.
Mammoth	A tape drive from Exabyte Corp.
master	A device capable of initiating a system bus (SBus) transaction. The term *CPU master* is used when a host CPU must be distinguished from a more generic SBus master. The term *DVMA master* is used when explicitly excluding CPU masters. Any SBus master may communicate with any other slave on the same bus, regardless of system configuration.
master backup server	A server that controls a group of backup servers.
master-of-masters server	A single centralized server that controls a group of master servers.
master-slave architecture	An architecture where master backup servers control slave backup servers. The slave servers perform the backup operations. (The data backed up may reside on the slave backup server, or on other servers across the network.)
mean-time-between-failures	The length of time between consecutive failures in the life of an item (under stated conditions).
Moving Picture Experts Group (MPEG)	This group has developed standards for compressing moving pictures and audio data and for synchronizing video and audio datastreams. The MPEG standard is similar to CCIT H.261 encoding, with compression rates in the range of 1-to-1.5 Mbits/sec. MPEG images are 352 by 240 pixels.
MPEG	See *Moving Picture Experts Group*

MTBF	See *mean-time-between-failures*
multiplexing	The process of backing up multiple streams of data (that may originate from a single or multiple data source) and directing the streams to one or more tape devices. The resulting tapes contain data in a "mixed up" format where data from one stream may be intermixed with data from another stream.
NAS	See *network attached storage*
NDMP	See *Network Data Management Protocol*
NetApp	See *Network Appliance*
Network Appliance	A company that makes specialized data server products.
NetBackup	See *Veritas NetBackup*
NetPerf	A benchmark used to measure the performance of different types of networks. It provides tests for both unidirectional throughput, and end-to-end latency.
Network Attached Storage (NAS)	Any storage device that is directly attached to a LAN.
Network Data Management Protocol (NDMP)	An open protocol for network based backup.
NetWorker	See *Legato Networker*
Network File System (NFS)	A technology developed by Sun Microsystems designed to give users high performance, transparent access to server file systems on global networks.
NFS	See *Network File System*
Oracle Enterprise Backup Utility (EBU)	High performance interface for backing up Oracle databases. Sometimes referred to as OEBU (for Oracle Enterprise Backup Utility).
Oracle Recovery Manager (RMAN)	High performance interface for backing up Oracle databases. RMAN is the Oracle8 equivalent of EBU.
Point-to-Point Protocol (PPP)	The successor to SLIP, PPP provides router-to-router and host-to-network connections over both synchronous and asynchronous circuits.
ProxyCopy	A feature in Oracle RMAN (available as of Oracle 8.1.5) that enables the backup tool to perform alternate backup methods while interacting with RMAN.
raw backup	A backup of an entire raw partition.

RAID	Redundant array of inexpensive disks. A subsystem for expanding disk storage.
remote procedure call (RPC)	An common paradigm for implementing the client-server model of distributed computing. A request sent to a remote system to execute a designated procedure using supplied arguments, with the results being returned to the caller. There are many variations of RPC, which have resulted in a variety of different protocols.
RMAN	The Oracle Recovery Manager, a high performance interface for backing up Oracle databases. RMAN is the Oracle8 equivalent of EBU.
RPC	See *remote procedure call*
runbook	A step-by-step procedure that describes how to use a specific software product.
SAN	See *storage area network*
SCSI	Small computer systems interface. An industry standard bus used to connect disk and tape devices to a workstation.
service level agreement (SLA)	A formalized agreement between an IT department and one of its customers that defines services provided, such as level of availability of computing resources.
SLA	See *service level agreement*
slave	An SBus device that responds with an acknowledgment to a slave select and address strobe signal. Any SBus master may communicate with any other slave on the same bus, regardless of system configuration.
slave backup server	A server that performs backup operations under the control of a master backup server.
SMP	See *symmetric multi-processing*
Solaris operating environment	An operating environment, from Sun Microsystems, Inc.
Solstice Backup	The Sun OEM version of the Legato Networker Backup tool.
Starfire	The Sun Enterprise 10000, a high-end SMP server that can scale to 64 processors and supports Dynamic System Domains for system partitioning.
Sun Enterprise E10000	Sun Enterprise 10000, also known as the Starfire.
STK	See *StorageTek*

storage area network (SAN)	High-speed dedicated network with a direct connection between storage devices and servers. This approach enables storage and tape subsystems to be connected remotely from a server. Tape SANs allow an efficient sharing of tape resources. Both the backup and restore tool and the tape library require SAN support to make this possible.
StorageTek (STK)	A company that provides network storage products.
symmetric multi-processing (SMP)	A method of using multiple processors in computer systems to deliver performance levels more predictable than MPP systems. SMP is efficient, and does not require specialized techniques for implementation.
Sun-Netscape Alliance	A business alliance between Sun Microsystems, Inc. and the Netscape division of AOL. See http://www.iplanet.com.
Sun StorEdge Enterprise NetBackUp	A backup tool. The Sun OEM version of VERITAS NetBackup.
SunUP	A collaborative program between Sun, customers and third parties to analyze, develop, implement and manage services, infrastructure, and products that improve availability. See http://www.sun.com/availability.
swap	Write the active pages of a job to external storage (swap space) and to read pages of another job from external page storage into real storage.
tape library	A hardware device that houses tapes, tape devices, and robotic tape loading devices.
temporal locality	The tendency for a program to reference the same memory locations over short time periods.
TCP	Transport control protocol. The major transport protocol in the Internet suite of protocols providing reliable, connection-oriented, full-duplex streams. This protocol uses IP for delivery.
True Image Restore	A feature of NetBackup that makes it possible to recreate data based on current allocations, negating the recovery of obsolete data.
vaulting	The process of storing backup media, such as tapes, at an offsite location.
VERITAS NetBackup	A backup tool from VERITAS. Sun distributes an OEM version of this product under the name Sun StorEdge Enterprise NetBackUp.
WAN	Wide-area network. A network consisting of many systems providing file transfer services. This type of network may cover a large physical area, sometimes spanning the globe.

Index

A

advances in backup technology, 20

age of tape drives (methodology), 74

alternate backup server support, selecting backup tool, 9

AME tape drive, 20

amount of data to be backed up, determining (methodology), 65

Andrew File System support, NetBackup (case study), 31

API support, NetBackup (case study), 32

application coverage, selecting backup tool, 13

applications to be backed up (case study), 56

architecting tape storage (case study), 37

architectural support, selecting backup tool, 6

architecture, benefits of new architecture (case study), 46

architecture, designing (case study), 33

architecture, tradeoffs in implementing new architecture (case study), 46

archive log backups, 44, 46

archive log backups management (case study), 57

ATL support, NetBackup (case study), 32

ATM performance, 84

atomicity of data, raw backups and, 67

automated backup and recovery procedures, 21

automated backup policies, 21

automatic multistreaming, 24
    all local drives command, 25
    new stream command, 25

automatic vs. manual backups (case study), 37

automation of recovery (case study), 47

automation support, selecting backup tool, 9

autonomy of clients (methodology), 70

AutoSys, PLATINUM Technology, 22

availability, 18

availability (case study), 28

availability support, selecting backup tool, 9

B

back-hitching, 69

backup architecture, planning (methodology), 63

backup policies, automated, 21

backup procedure (NetBackup Runbook), 119

backup progress status, selecting backup tool, 8

backup schedule, default (case study), 36

backup schedule, example table (case study), 59

backup schedules (case study), 52

backup schedules, database (case study), 45

backup server vs. data server issues (methodology), 68

backup servers, are they distributed (methodology), 75

backup speed, selecting backup tool, 10

backup time vs. recovery time (case study), 37

backup tool selection, 6

backup tool selection (case study), 31

backup tool vendor relationship (case study), 30

backup window (methodology), 76

backups
    advances in backup technology, 20

C

customization ease, selecting backup tool, 12

D

data compression, 23, 79

data compression ratios, 80

data criticality (case study), 34

data local to backup server (methodology), 75

data origin issues (methodology), 68

data server vs. backup server issues (methodology), 68

data servers, are they distributed (methodology), 75

data streams
    automatic multistreaming, 24
    demultiplexing tapes, 23
    multiplexing, 22, 54
    multiplexing, when to use (case study), 40
    RMAN, 21

data type and compression, determining
    (methodology), 66

data unavailability, is it acceptable (methodology), 77

data, amount of data to be backed up (methodology), 65

data, how is it laid out (methodology), 70

data, how much must be backed up (methodology), 77

database
    archive log backups, 44, 46
    backup schedules (case study), 45
    data recovery vs. database recovery, 42
    database backup strategy (case study), 57
    database backups, hot vs. exports (case study), 42
    database backups, overview, 18
    database compression ratio, 66
    database coverage, selecting backup tool, 13
    database table-level backup support, selecting
      backup tool, 11
    exports (case study), 43
    hot backup process, Oracle, 43
    Oracle Enterprise Backup Utility (EBU), 19
    Oracle parallel export script, 139
    Oracle Recovery Manager (RMAN), 19, 21
    roll forward mode, 44

datacenter initiatives at Sun, 1

datacenter using Sun enterprise servers (case study), 28

datacenter.com, 2

dataset size, determining (methodology), 64

DBAs and system administrators, working together, 5

default backup schedule (case study), 36

deleting progress logs (NetBackup Runbook), 135

demultiplexing tapes, 23

designing new architecture (case study), 33

differential backups, 77

Direct I/O, 68

disaster recovery, 159

disaster recovery support, selecting backup tool, 8

disasters, minimize impact of (methodology), 78

disk bandwidth issues (methodology), 69

disk recovery time, selecting backup tool, 10

disk subsystem issues (methodology), 70

disks, capabilities of (methodology), 72

disks, how are they arranged into volumes
    (methodology), 71

disks, how are they managed (methodology), 71

distribution of clients (methodology), 70

distribution of tape drives (methodology), 73

DLT4000, 20

DLT7000, 73

documentation clarity, selecting backup tool, 11

dumps, fully-consistent, 18

E

E10000, 2

EBU, 19, 36

enterprise servers in datacenter (case study), 28

enterprise, understanding (methodology), 64

equipment loss, is it critical to minimize impact of
    (methodology), 78

error messages, selecting backup tool, 11

errors, is it critical to minimize impact of
    (methodology), 78

Ethernet performance, 84

event-based schedulers, 22

EXB-8900, 73

export script, 139

exports, Oracle (case study), 43

F

failed job restart support, selecting backup tool, 10

FastEthernet performance, 84

FDDI performance, 84

file structure issues (methodology), 67